POP MYTHOLOGY:

COLLECTED ESSAYS

by

Laura A. Shamas

If you purchased this book without a cover you should be aware that this book is stolen property. It was reported as "unsold and destroyed" to the publisher and neither the author nor the publisher has received any payment for this "stripped book."

This book is a work of non-fiction. The author has used a variety of sources to complete this book. While all information is believed to be correct, neither the author nor the publisher provide any warranties, either expressed or implied, about its accuracy.

POP MYTHOLOGY: COLLECTED ESSAYS
Copyright © 2012 by Laura Shamas. All rights reserved, including the right to reproduce this book, or portions thereof, in any form. No part of this text may be reproduced, transmitted, downloaded, decompiled, reverse engineered, or stored in or introduced into any information storage and retrieval system, in any form or by any means, whether electronic or mechanical without the express written permission of the author. The scanning, uploading, and distribution of this book via the Internet or via any other means without the permission of the publisher is illegal and punishable by law. Please purchase only authorized electronic editions and do not participate in or encourage electronic piracy of copyrighted materials.

The publisher does not have any control over and does not assume any responsibility for author or third-party websites or their content.

Cover Designed by Ty Donaldson

Cover Art: Copyright © Ty Donaldson
www.buddhacowboy.com

Visit the author website:
http://www.Laurashamas.com

ISBN: 978-1-938135-22-4 (eBook)
ISBN: 978-1-938135-23-1 (paperback)

Version 2012.07.16

Printed in the United States of America

10 9 8 7 6 5 4 3 2 1

The following essays are reprinted with permission:

"Aphrodite and Ecology: The Goddess of Love as Nature Archetype" was originally published in *EcoPsychology*. 2009: 1:93-97.

"Apollo Updated: Zero Effect": This essay was originally published in *The San Francisco Jung Institute Library Journal* (Now *Jung Journal: Culture and Psyche*), November 2000, Volume 19, Number 3, Pages 71-79. ©2000 by *San Francisco Jung Institute Library Journal*.

"Unseen Beauty: Artemis and Dark Matter" was originally published in *Mythopoetry Scholar*, Volume 2, "Matter and Beauty." Mythopoetry.com, January 2, 2011. http://www.mythopoetry.com/mythopoetics/scholar11_shamas_artemis.html.

"Understanding the Myth: Why Cassandra Must Not Be Silenced." This essay was originally published in *On The Issues Magazine*, The Café, Summer 2011, on July 13, 2011. http://www.ontheissuesmagazine.com/2011summer/.

"The Hera Factor in Hillary's Run" was originally published in *The Los Angeles Times* on July 11, 1999, pages M3 & M6.

"The Holiness of Health" was originally published in *Mythopoetry Scholar*, Volume 1, "Health and Well-Being." Mythopoetry.com, January 2, 2010. http://mythopoetry.com/mythopoetics/scholar09_shamas.html.

"Muse-Worthy: Francine Prose's *The Lives of the Muses*" by Laura A. Shamas was first published in "The Muses," *Spring Journal* 70, March 2004, pages 15-23. Website: springjournalandbooks.com.

"America's Zeus" was originally published in *Newsday* on January 14, 2001, with the title "The Clinton Years: America's Zeus," page B5.

"The Gaming of Love" was originally published with the title "Love Might Hurt But We Still Like to Watch," *The Los Angeles Times*, August 8, 2000, p. F3.

"End Times: Old Problem, New Myth" was originally published with the title "Old Problem, New Myth: Y2K hype latest manifestation of humanity's resistance to change" in *The Los Angeles Daily News*, Viewpoint, Sunday, June 20, 1999 (p. 3).

"Revolution and the *I Ching*: A Meditation on Hexagram 49" was originally published in *Mythopoetry Scholar*, Volume Three: "Revolution." January 2, 2012, with the title "Revolution and the *I Ching*: Hexagram 49 Reflections." http://www.mythopoetry.com/mythopoetics/sch12_shamas_essay.html.

"The Trickster and the President" was originally published as "Clinton's Transformation Into Mythical Trickster," Opinion Section, *The Los Angeles Times*, February 7, 1999. Pages M2 and M6.

Sections of "Hero Worship and the Academy Awards" were originally published in the *2004 Society for Interdisciplinary Study of Social Imagery (SISSI) Conference Proceedings: The Image of the Hero in Literature, Media and Society* with the title: "Oscar Exemplars: Towards an Exploration of Current Heroes, Hero Worship, and the Academy Awards."

"Movies and Creation Myth—*2001: A Space Odyssey*" was originally published on the "C.G. Jung Page" in January 2001. Cgjungpage.org.

"Entertainment: The Meaning of the Word and Ritual" was originally published as "'Entertainment': A Dirty Word?" Calendar Section, *The Los Angeles Times*, May 1, 2000.

"On the Fortieth Anniversary of Title IX: Female Athletes in Sacred Stories" was originally published with the title "Leaping, Racing, Spearing: The Female Athlete Amazes in Myth" in *On The Issues Magazine*, Spring 2012, on April 18, 2012. Ontheissuesmagazine.com.

TABLE OF CONTENTS

INTRODUCTION   i

PART ONE—PANTHEON PIECES

1) APHRODITE—Aphrodite and Ecology:
   The Goddess of Love as Nature Archetype   1
2) APOLLO—Apollo Updated: *Zero Effect*   14
3) ARTEMIS—Unseen Beauty: Artemis and Dark Matter   26
4) ATHENA—Pieces of Athena (and Her Head)   32
5) CASSANDRA—Understanding the Myth:
   Why Cassandra Must Not Be Silenced   42
6) HERA—The Hera Factor in Hillary's Run   47
7) HESTIA—Martha Hearts Hestia   50
8) HYGIEIA & AESCLEPIUS—The Holiness of Health   59
9) THE MUSES—Muse-Worthy:
   Francine Prose's *The Lives of the Muses*   66
10) ZEUS—America's Zeus   75

PART TWO—MYTH MISCELLANY

11) The Gaming of Love   81
12) End Times: Old Problem, New Myth   85
13) Revolution and the *I Ching*: A Meditation on
    Hexagram 49   89
14) The Trickster and The President   100
15) Hero Worship and the Academy Awards   104
16) Movies and Creation Myth—*2001: A Space Odyssey*   110
17) Entertainment: The Meaning of the Word and Ritual   117

18) Acts of Protest, Athena, and *Lysistrata*	120
19) Matters of the Heart and Soul: Courtly Love	131
20) Facing the Dragon: Of Presidential Nominees and Acceptance Speeches	142
21) A Few Thoughts on Adaptation	163
22) Swimming In the Tweet Stream	180
23) On the Fortieth Anniversary of Title IX: Female Athletes in Sacred Stories	185
ACKNOWLEDGEMENTS	193
LIST OF ORIGINAL PUBLICATIONS/PRESENTATIONS FOR ESSAYS	194

"No human society has yet been found in which such mythological motifs have not been rehearsed in liturgies; interpreted by seers, poets, theologians or philosophers; presented in art; magnified in song; and ecstatically experienced in life-empowering visions."
 —Joseph Campbell, Introduction, *The Mask of the Gods, Volume 1 (Primitive Mythology)*, page 3 (1959)

"...contemporary pop culture is a source of images just as relevant for amplification as any other source. By images in popular culture, I mean any images currently in pervasive cultural circulation, including those in mass media such as movies."
 —Michael Vannoy Adams, *The Mythological Unconscious*, page 180 (2001)

POP MYTHOLOGY:
COLLECTED ESSAYS

INTRODUCTION

This collection of essays represents the various ways I've worked with mythology in the past few years. It is not a theoretical book per se, nor does it aim to explain the power of myth. It is, rather, a documentation of my work with myth in the twenty-first century as a writer, teacher and speaker; it reflects aspects of my work as a myth consultant in business and entertainment. It chronicles my journey as a cultural mythologist with a media specialty.

When I was ten years old, I sat at a typewriter in Tulsa, Oklahoma, and from our family den, pecked out a one-pager every month called "Shamas News." After my father Xeroxed it for me, I distributed this sheet to friends and family. That same fascination with "news" inspired me, as an adult, to co-create a mythology/news website years later. In 2000, my brother Jimmy Shamas and I launched "HeadlineMuse.com." We published essays by talented, erudite scholars and writers about mythology, related to varied facets of contemporary life and culture worldwide. At the same time, I listed the website and my credentials on a private press database, and spoke to nearly every reporter who asked for an expert quote about possible mythic intersections with events, news, culture, and trends. I was quoted about myth in news stories published by ABC News.com, *Amusement Business, The Associated Press, The Austin American-Statesman, The Baltimore Sun,* CNET.com, *The*

Chicago Sun-Times, ChickClick.com, *The Cleveland Plain Dealer, The Dallas Morning News, The Denver Post*, FoxNews.com (NY), *The Fresno Bee, The Hamilton Spectator* (Canada), *The Hartford Courant, The Los Angeles Times*, MyPrimeTime.com, *The St. Petersburg Times, The Sacramento Bee*, and *The Seattle Times*.

I began to write editorials or OpEds with myth-related content for newspapers, such as *The Los Angeles Times* and *Newsday*. I'd request that HeadlineMuse.com be listed in my quotes or credentials with the news stories, in order to bring free publicity to the site; we were always trying to expand our readership. We had momentum or "buzz" for a time, although the website was never financially profitable. For several years, reporters seeking myth-related quotes continued to contact me from the United States and Canada.

At one point, a television producer wrote to me about creating a possible show in which I would be the "expert pop culture commentator." Later, a talk show production assistant asked me if I could create a dictionary with a correlation of current social issues to specific examples in mythology, so that archetypal commentary could possibly be included in their show on a regular basis. I had a radio in-studio audition, in Los Angeles, about myth, pop culture, and the news. I learned much about mythology in the trying. Headline Muse ended in 2007, and I kept writing and speaking about myth.

How and why did the human psyche develop a need for "news?" Did our desire for it begin when our ancestors sat around a nighttime cave campfire, with the tribal elder or shaman, exchanging stories about what they had seen in the world that day? Or when the town crier was paid to spread the king's word by ringing a bell to signal the community to gather round? In English, the word "news" is derived from the Middle English "newes" which meant "new things, tidings." "Journalism" comes from old

French and Latin words meaning "daily." These words are etymological indications that the "news" should offer daily stories that connect to community. But make no mistake, through "news," we are connecting via story. You can tell it with video and graphs, shouting pundits and crawls, but those are just the postmodern tools to deliver tales of the day. News involves the re-telling of stories, something connected to mythology as well.

This volume represents a selected collection of my essays published from 1999–2012 in newspapers, journals, and electronic media. A few are based on papers I presented at academic conferences, or talks I gave at universities. It is a varied, eclectic collection of myth miscellany, ranging from informal articles to "OpEds" to scholarly essays. In most essays, I have kept the original citation system as required by each publication, so there is "style" variety throughout. My interests are interdisciplinary in scope, intersecting mythological, film, theater, literary and cultural studies. I am also introducing some new essays in this volume.

Each essay begins with a brief annotation explaining its original publication or incarnation, and contextualization if applicable. In some essays, the popular culture references are out of date and might seem irrelevant. But if patterns of human behavior are observable, there is value in them still. I have annotated each of them in an effort to enhance their continued viability.

There are scholars who rightly continue to debate the value or relevancy of myth in the twenty-first century, who identify the misinterpretation and misapplication of ancient myth to contemporary issues and situations, based on a variety of astute criticisms ranging from (and not limited to): 1) a lack of authentic modern/postmodern understanding of the meaning of religion, including rites, rituals and symbols, to ancient peoples; 2) the failure of facile how-to "psychologizations" of mythology and archetypes; 3) the popularized entertainment appropriation and dilution of specific myths or the use of myth theories as cookie-cutter screenwriting templates; 4) the temporality of Myth (here/gone—and therefore obsolete); 5) to elusory definitions of what is and what is not myth, etc. I will continue to read and consider mythological scholarship, which I find fascinating, engaging, and challenging.

However, in my opinion, mythology and its related imagery continue to be part of our cultural zeitgeist, and therefore relevant, as we see in hit movies about mythic heroes, or brief references made in unexpected ways, such as in the *glitterati* of celebrity culture. In 2011, for example, a major television star, going through a public "meltdown," referred to his two female lovers as "the goddesses," and bragged about his "Adonis DNA."[1] This, to me, was truly "pop mythology."

And we "mythologize" our celebrities. As author Chris Hedges writes in his bestselling 2009 critique of American culture, *Empire of Illusion: The End of Literacy and the Triumph of Spectacle*: "And in American society our gods are celebrities. Religious belief and practice are commonly transferred to the adoration of celebrities. Our culture builds temples to celebrities the way Romans did for divine emperors, ancestors, and household gods. We are a *de facto* polytheistic society. We engage in the same kind of primitive beliefs as older polytheistic cultures. In celebrity culture, the object is to get as close as possible to the celebrity. Relics of celebrities are coveted as magical talismans."[2]

Story transmission continues to evolve in the twenty-first century; it is now dispersed through social media channels online and via a myriad of electronic devices, in addition to more traditional media such as print, radio and television. I am interested in learning if or how social media affects our understanding of myth.

Although many examples in these essays center on figures from the Greek or Roman pantheons used as a shorthand in terms of myth/archetypal familiarity based on standard Western educational practices (such as in Part One, "Pantheon Pieces"), I remain extremely interested in comparative mythology and traditions worldwide (such as is found in Part Two, "Myth Miscellany"). My first exposure to myth was not rooted in Greek or Roman tradition. My last name, "Shamas," is derived from the sun god Shamash, a character in the epic Gilgamesh cycle, from Assyrian-Babylonian-Sumerian traditions. My initial experience of studying epic legends was reading *Beowulf* in the fourth grade in Tulsa. Perhaps that locates my earliest mythic interests as Middle Eastern/Anglo-Saxon—by way of Oklahoma. My dissertation about Shakespeare's Weird Sisters and female trios in myth and fairy tales (*"We Three": The Mythology of Shakespeare's Weird Sisters*, 2007) partially reflects the roots of my love of myth and folklore, as do some of the other articles in this collection.

In these pages, you'll encounter Aphrodite, Apollo, Artemis, Athena, Cassandra, Hera, Hestia, Hygieia and Aesclepius, the Muses, Zeus, Hermes, the Apocalypse, a legendary King, a Tiger, a Panther, the Trickster, the Hero/the Heroine, Janus, Lysistrata, the Knight and the Troubadour (*amour courtois*), the Python/Dragon, the Amazons, Mazu, The Woman, and Oya. I hope you'll be invigorated and inspired by them.

–Laura A. Shamas
February 5, 2012

---

[1] Charlie Sheen, February 18, 2011. http://www.cbsnews.com/2300-504083_162-10006865.html. Also: http://www.cbsnews.com/8301-31749_162-20037296-10391698.html.

[2] Hedges, Chris. *Empire of Illusion: The End of Literacy and the Triumph of Spectacle*. New York: Nation Books, 2009. Page 17.

PART ONE: PANTHEON PIECES

1) APHRODITE
Aphrodite and Ecology: The Goddess of Love as Nature Archetype

(Note: This essay was first published in EcoPsychology Journal, Volume One, Number 2, June 2009. Pages 93–97. Its first draft was written in 1999.)

Introduction

"Ah Muse, tell me about the things Aphrodite does, the golden one, the Cyprian one, she who awakens a pleasant yearning in gods, she who subdues the race of mortal men, and the birds of Zeus, and all the many animals that the land nourishes, and the sea nourishes. The works of the beautifully crowned Cytherean are the concern of all these."

– "The Hymn to Aphrodite," The Homeric Hymns

At the intersection of mythological studies and ecopsychology, the huntress-goddess Artemis from the Olympian pantheon is often referenced as a key female nature symbol, mythologically expressive of the "active feminine" principle connected to conservation and wildlife; conservation historian J. Donald Hughes (1994) writes that Artemis "might be seen as an early patron of environmental education" (p. 94). Jungians and archetypalists have promoted "Artemistic purity and self-sufficiency" (Moore, 1994, p. 99) as a symbol of our planet's natural resources and their self-renewing processes. Gaia, from the pre-Titan pantheon, has long been referenced as a mythic symbol for "Mother Earth," as C. G. Jung (1956) did in *Symbols of Transformation* (p. 182). "Gaia" is popularly used as a metaphor for earth by scientists and activists alike.

Aphrodite has largely been excluded from our top lists of nature-related archetypes in depth psychology and ecopsychology. It is time we rediscover the Goddess of Love's ancient resonance as a powerful nature figure and consider what value this archetype may hold for ecopsychology in the 21st century. A closer reexamination of her myths and cult reveals Aphrodite as representing nature's fertility, and symbolic new life and regeneration through myriad natural images of oceans, mountains, islands, animals, plants, and planets.

The Relevance of Myth

Archetypes, such as Aphrodite, represent, in a Jungian sense, a collective, inherited, unconscious pattern of human behavior, thought, or image. This concept is related to the idea of a "first imprint" or "model." Mythologists define a pantheon as an assemblage of gods and goddesses, usually grouped together by region and/or era; from the perspective of depth psychology, a pantheon can be seen to represent a collection of various patterns of behaviors and/or images that have universal relevance. As ancient gods and goddesses were figures of religious worship, aspects of spirituality are also present in archetypes, related to divinity and the concept of "soul" or sacred essence. Myths may be perceived as special stories that show us something of the past—but they may also give us glimpses of the future, as the "perpetual truth" in these legends has survived for millennia. As Theodore Roszak (1992) writes in

The Voice of the Earth, myths "have the immortality of the phoenix. Reduced to ashes, they undergo miraculous transformations, returning to life with their essence intact" (p. 137). The application of aspects of myth and depth psychology have been integrated into ecopsychology in various ways, including the metaphoric use of archetypes in therapies, rituals, and education.

There are many reminders of the power of Aphrodite's connection to nature in the ways in which she was worshipped long ago. As James Hillman (1975) writes in *Re-Visioning Psychology*, Aphrodite's true essence is embodied in "the locations of her temples...her festivals and her favorite landscapes, localities, animals, plants" (p. 184), natural elements related to geography, earth, flora, and fauna. Homer identified the Goddess of Love's procreative powers over plants and animals (Friedrich, 1978, p. 99). Recognizing the sacrality of nature, seeding, and regeneration are vital psychic steps needed to restore our planet's natural vibrancy.

Aphrodite's primordial relationship to nature symbology and the concept of new life and renewal may be seen through an examination of the following: the evolution of her archetype and its various fertility/animal associations; her ties to the life-giving sea and oceanic images such as seashells and foam; Aphrodite's "green thumb" and her powerful effect on plants and formal gardens in Athens; her connection to the seasons; Aphroditic links to "beautiful places" on earth (e.g., seashores, islands, and mountains); and how her archetype is part of our understanding of the universe and astronomy.

Birth of a Goddess

The history of Aphrodite's archetype is directly relevant to her iconographic presence; nature was part of her mythic persona from the start. The goddess of love has multicultural origins: most likely a combination of the Sumerian Inanna, the Semitic Ishtar, the

Phoenician Astarte, the Old European "Bird Goddess," the Minoan "Dove Goddess," and the Early Greek Eos (Dawn), all of whom eventually converged and were constellated to the Greek goddess Aphrodite (Friedrich, 1978, p. 52). Later, she was also known by her Roman name, Venus.

Clearly, birds were essential to the image of Aphrodite, as they were part of the identifying image/appellation of her goddess progenitors in two cultures. Doves were also probably linked to Ishtar. Astarte was associated with the image of the cow. Both doves and cows symbolize fertility.

Eggs—a primal image tied to birds—are also part of the procreative energy as emblematized by birds/doves, inherent in the archetype of Bird Goddess. This is key to Aphrodite's early mythological power; eggs themselves are important nature symbols, signifying earth, new life, or the seat of the soul. Hyginus, a mythographer writing in Latin in the 2nd century C.E., reported that Aphrodite herself was born from an egg that mysteriously appeared in a river (Grigson, 1977, p. 33). Thus, Aphrodite's early and later iterations evoked psychic images of earth, life, and soul; this was synthesized and well-established in her archetypal resonance by the time she became fully "Greek."

Water—The Beginning

The stories of Aphrodite were transmitted via trade routes used by sea merchants beginning in the 13th century B.C.E. (Grigson, 1977, pp. 30–31). Aphrodite's image was always linked to the ocean; according to Geoffrey Grigson in *The Goddess of Love*, the Greeks "supposed that the first syllable of their mispronounced name for her was their own aphros, 'foam'" (p. 31).

Water is the beginning of life for all species on earth, amniotic fluid and the ocean are the vessels for human birth and all other life forms. Aphrodite's major image is that of the life-giving ocean—of the sea and the womb. The sea was the focus of one of her key myths. According to Hesiod, Uranus was Aphrodite's father. She came from one of the testicles of her father, one that was cut off by Cronos and thrown into the sea. White foam swelled there, and a maiden was formed. Sea foam, too, evokes images of white, salty wetness, which has been tied to the idea of sperm, another life force. There is evidence that Aphrodite's cult honored her with rites involving cakes of salt, which stood for the Goddess of Love's sea birth (Grigson, 1977, p. 41). Jane Ellen Harrison (1991), in her *Prolegomena to the Study of Greek Religion*, finds proof of "ritual Bath and the Sea-birth" as part of Aphrodite's rites as well, which served as periodic ceremonial renewals of her virginity (p. 311). Thus baths, with their therapeutic rejuvenating waters representing her ocean birth, also became part of Aphrodite's rites.

Seashells have long been a symbol affiliated with Aphrodite. Artistic representations of her, dating from as early as the 5th century B.C.E., depict the Goddess of Love's birth as an emanation from a seashell (Grigson, 1977, p. 37). Sandro Botticelli's "Birth of Venus," created during the Italian Renaissance, is an update of those ancient representations. Carolyn Merchant (1980), in *The Death of Nature*, interprets Botticelli's seashell Aphroditic image as depicting fertility (p. 8).

From Water to Earth

Andrew Dalby (2005) writes in *Venus: A Biography* that as soon as the Goddess of Love set foot on land, grass was fertilized: "Here she stepped ashore, and grass and flowers grew beneath her tender feet as she walked" (p. 13).

The rose, as is so beautifully shown in Botticelli's "Birth of Venus," was one of Aphrodite's flowers; the myrtle was the other. But she was the goddess who made all plants grow to maturity, as if she had a "green thumb." John Sanford (1995), in *Fate, Love and*

Ecstasy: Wisdom from the Lesser-Known Goddesses of the Greeks, notes: "Less well known is the influence of Aphrodite over all natural life. It was said, for instance, that while the goddess Demeter caused all things to grow, it was Aphrodite who caused the flowers to ripen. For this reason, gardens and flowers were sacred to the goddess—especially the rose, which, with its deep colors and voluptuous, inviting blossoms, was regarded as a holy and unique expression of the essence of the goddess of love herself" (p. 8).

Barbara Walker (1988) sees the Aphroditic rose as the basis for Christian use of the flower as a religious symbol, related to fertility and the giving of life: "Worshippers of Aphrodite used to call their ceremonies the Mysteries of the Rose. Even medieval churchmen understood that the rose was a physical gateway, source of the Redeemer's life" (pp. 12–13).

Aphrodite was also associated with the seasons and, therefore, ruled over some aspects of agriculture. According to Hesiod's account of her birth myth, the Horai (The Hours/The Seasons) were the first to greet her after she arose from the sea; they covered her with garments and a golden crown. It is from the mention of gold in Hesiod and Homer that Aphrodite is most often associated with the sun; this part of her birth myth shows that the seasons and time supported Aphrodite's dictates. The seasons attended her; they are part of her domain (Friedrich, 1978, p. 52). The seasons are earth's cycles of life; regenerative associations are made to the coming of spring, which, mythologically, has always been Persephone's realm—but Aphrodite controls the entire life cycle of the planet: not only spring, but summer, fall, and winter, too. In Athens and Attica, she was known sometimes as Aphrodite en Kepois or "Aphrodite of the Gardens" (Rosenzweig, 2004, p. 4). Aphrodite en Kepois was so important to Athens that there were three shrines there connected to her fertility aspects (Rosenzweig, 2004, p. 45).

Aphrodite was linked to gardens through the archetype of Adonis as well. In *Worshipping Aphrodite: Art and Cult in Classical Athens*, Rachel Rosenzweig (2004) details some of the ritual elements of the ancient Adonia Festival. In June or July, Athenian females seeded plants such as barley, fennel, lettuce, and wheat to grow "Gardens of Adonis" in jars, pots, and baskets. In the intense summer heat, the plants would shrivel and die before reaching true maturity—like Adonis, god of youthful beauty. Women mounted ladders, bringing the "Gardens of Adonis" vessels to Athenian rooftops as part of the ritual; up there nearer the heavens, and with food and wine, the ladies mourned the dying plants, just as Aphrodite grieved after gorgeous Adonis died. Aphrodite was depicted on Athenian vase paintings in the late classical era as climbing a ladder carrying a "Gardens of Adonis" vessel, planted with sprouting seeds (Rosenzweig, 2004, p. 46). In other parts of Greece and Asia, the Gardens of Adonis containers were cast into the sea as part of the ritual; 7 days later, the red anemone bloomed (Leach, 1972), signaling regeneration and cyclic renewal.

Jung (1956) notes in *Symbols of Transformation* that "in antiquity mint was called 'Aphrodite's crown.'" Jung cites Apuleius' use of the term "mentha venerea," a sign that the mint plant was thought to have aphrodisiacal properties (p. 146)—yet another herbal association between the Goddess of Love and fertility.

Cult evidence shows that Aphrodite was linked to other natural habitats, which were scenic and beautiful—not just the ocean's shores. Fruits, birds, and cosmological forces were also significant to her rites. Paul Friedrich, in *The Meaning of Aphrodite* (1978), traces the Love Goddess' ties to islands and mountains (p. 73), where various shrines to Aphrodite aided sea navigation and provided inspiration to sailors (Grigson, 1977, p. 49). Apples were sacred to the Love Goddess. Creation myths and the Bible depict the apple as a symbol of the beginning of life, knowledge, and original sin— yet more reproductive allusions associated with Aphrodite. Birds were sacred to her, as previously mentioned (related to the earlier Bird and Dove goddesses), especially swans and doves.

From Earth to Sky: Heavenly Beacon

In terms of cosmology, the sun and moon were part of her rites—the sun, because Aphrodite came from a sky god, and the moon, because of astral references related to Inanna, the Phoenician Astarte, and Eos, earlier goddesses who were incorporated into her Greek archetypal resonance (Friedrich, 1978, pp. 79–80). The sun and moon represent more cycles of time: of the day, of the night, of life.

The planet Venus is a nighttime and astronomical presence for the goddess as well—an important one. As Tamra Andrews (1998) writes of the planets in *A Dictionary of Nature Myths*, the planet Venus "moved the most obviously and it always stayed close to the sun. Except for the sun and the moon, Venus is the brightest object in the sky" (p. 131). Andrews notes that ancient astronomers charted "the dual nature" of Venus' bright rhythms; they saw a parallel between Venus rising above the horizon to Venus rising from the ocean in her birth myth. Andrews also traces Venus' planetary value as a key astronomical–mythological signifier in cultures worldwide, as in the stories of goddess Auszrine in Slavic and Russian mythologies, and as in the Hindu mythology tales of the Aswin twins, who represent the morning and evening stars (p. 131).

Joanne H. Stroud (1996), in "Aphrodite and the Ensouled World," discusses a drawing of Keith Critchlow's as "a remarkable pentagonal diagram of the planetary pattern that the planet Venus takes in the heavens, entering and leaving" (p. 106).

The planet Venus was also important long ago as a steadying reference point for nighttime sailing—especially for long voyages. Stroud (1996) points out: "Aphrodite does relate to the rhythm of the tides" (p. 106). And so the sky is connected to the ocean through her archetype.

Applications

According to the Fifth Homeric Hymn, as cited in the Introduction, Aphrodite is nearly the mistress of all realms: natural, human, and divine. In *Worshipping Aphrodite*, Rosenzweig (2004) observes that, in Athens, "as Aphrodite en Kepois (Aphrodite of the Gardens), her powers of fertility extended to all forms of life, including people, animals and vegetation" (p. 4). Doves, eggs, water, sea, seashells, salt, foam, baths, roses, myrtles, the seasons, the color gold, gardens, islands, mountains, apples, swans, the sun, the moon, a planet/star: these are natural elements associated with Aphrodite's divinity that resonate symbolically with creation—reproduction/regeneration—issues in ecology and ecopsychology.

Much more than just a lascivious deity of love and sex, or the goddess known for the power of her jealous wrath when crossed, Aphrodite is the Olympian goddess who ensures that new life is created, that regeneration occurs, that a seed can grow. The Goddess of Love's archetypal resonance intersects two key ecological elements referenced in prominent climate discussions of the 21st century: water and sun.

What if acknowledging Aphrodite's powerful archetypal resonance as an ecopsychological psychic image could help to facilitate new life and regenerative healing on a grand level in the twenty-first century?

Specifically, Aphrodite could be of value as a metaphorical and inspirational figure in ecopsychological therapies and in education. Something as simple as a daily meditation on a budding rose plant, which would encourage a deeper connection to the cycle of flowering and blooming, could be seen as an Aphrodite-inspired activity. The organic care of an apple orchard, with a conscious awareness of the white budding blossoms which grow to juicy fruits and whose seeds return to the earth again, could also be seen as a beautiful Aphroditic sequence of events. A seashore (Aphrodite's birthplace) is a potent therapeutic setting, where humans can appreciate the liminality of water touching land. A beach or lake's edge may inspire us to begin to be more aware of the earth, of the purifying, baptismal force of lapping water on its shores, and as a place where generation and fertility is sourced. Activities such as "coastal clean-ups" also may be categorized as related to Aphrodite—as a way to return the coast to its original beautiful state.

It is possible to encourage the use of something as functional as a solar-powered water heater and to reference it metaphorically as related to Aphrodite birth myth and a love of the earth. Aphrodite was a sun goddess, birthed in oceanic maternal waters before arriving on the beach fully grown—as an image of fertilizing Love. Aphrodite is especially relatable, symbolically, to issues that encompass solar power, water power, fertility, and a love of earth.

Growing a sustainable garden through the seasons may be categorized under Aphrodite's archetypal umbrella, due to her influence on the ripening of the flowers and her affect on the seasons. Enjoying the restorative beauty of a garden is also under the Goddess of Love's domain.

Ecotherapy courses whose topics include grief and despair about environmental issues may find an effective use of aspects of the "Gardens of Adonis" ritual, which in ancient times commemorated Aphrodite's grief about the death of beautiful Adonis. The floating gardens, so significant in this ritual, came to emblematize renewal and regeneration, and nature's cyclicity. Perhaps a modern re-imagining of this ritual could prove useful in coping with grief about the environment.

The psychic potential of Aphrodite's archetypal presence may be engaged any time a creative link exists between nature's beauty, fertility, and love of the earth.

Conclusion

Ecopsychologist Theodore Roszak (1995), in "Where Psyche Meets Gaia," correlates the condition of the human psyche to the planet's outer physical climate: "Toxic wastes, the depletion of resources, the annihilation of our fellow species; all these speak to us, if we would hear, of our deep self" (p. 5). This gives even more reason for us to explore the possibilities of healing inherent in the Goddess of Love's image. Aphrodite embodies a vision of new life and regeneration *in toto*; as Thomas Moore (1998) notes in *The Soul of Sex*, "Aphrodite's body is the archetype of the human body and also of the body of the world" (p. 21). Jung (1956), in *Symbols and Transformations*, writes that in Orphic mythology, Aphrodite is the center of the world, alongside Hecate and Gaia, a key to "the world-soul itself" (p. 370).

The archetype of Aphrodite offers us a chance for the new and renewal—a path to heal the dysfunctional relationship between the environment and humans—through creation and regeneration. We must add her back to our canon of ecology archetypes in ecopsychology. Coastal/maritime purity, animal and insect extinction, removal of pollution, land conservation and revivification, wild habitat preservation, water conservation, related agricultural issues (as in use of pesticides, growing cycles), global warming (which indicates a world out of Aphrodite balance related to the sun): these are but a few of the major modern ecological issues that could be positively affected by our response to nature aspects of Aphrodite's archetypal resonance.

Aphrodite serves as a loving bridge between the natural world and the human psyche. It is time to honor nature aspects of Aphrodite again—for nature's sake and our own. The planet longs for the divinity of her eternal flowering. As the poet of *Cypria*[3] once described the Goddess of Love's appearance:

"She clothed herself with garments which the Graces and Hours had once made for her and dyed in flowers of spring—such flowers as the Seasons wear—in crocus and hyacinth and flourishing violet and rose's lovely bloom, so sweet and delicious, and heavenly buds, the flowers of the narcissus and lily. In such perfumed garments is Aphrodite clothed at all seasons."

REFERENCES

Andrews, T. (1998). *A Dictionary of Nature Myths: Legends of the Earth, Sea and Sky*. Oxford: Oxford University Press.

"[The] Hymn To Aphrodite." *Homeric Hymns, The*. (1970). (C. Boer, Trans., Rev. 2nd ed, pp. 69–80). Woodstock, CT: Spring.

Dalby, A. (2005). *Venus: A Biography*. Los Angeles: Getty.

Friedrich, P. (1978). *The Meaning of Aphrodite*. Chicago: University of Chicago Press.

Grigson, G. (1977). *The Goddess of Love*. New York: Stein and Day.

Harrison, J. E. (1991). *Prologemena to the Study of Greek Religion*. Princeton, NJ: Princeton University Press.

Hillman, J. (1975). *Re-Visioning Psychology*. New York: HarperPerennial.

Hughes, J. D. (1994). *Pan's Travail: Environmental Problems of the Ancient Greeks and Romans*. Baltimore: Johns Hopkins University Press.

Jung, C. G. (1956). *Symbols of Transformation* (R. F. C. Hull, Trans., Bollingen Series, XX. Vol. 5). Princeton, NJ: Princeton University Press.

Leach, M. (Ed.). (1972). *Funk and Wagnalls Standard Dictionary of Folklore, Mythology and Legend.* San Francisco: Harper San Francisco.

Merchant, C. (1980). *The Death of Nature.* San Francisco: Harper San Francisco.

Moore, T. (1994). *Care of the Soul.* New York: HarperPerennial.

Moore, T. (1998). *The Soul of Sex.* New York: Harper Collins.

Rosenzweig, R. (2004). *Worshipping Aphrodite: Art and Cult in Classical Athens.* Ann Arbor, MI: University of Michigan Press.

Roszak, T. (1992). *The Voice of the Earth: An Exploration of Ecopsychology.* Grand Rapids, MI: Phanes Press.

Roszak, T. (1995). "Where Psyche Meets Gaia." In T. Roszak, M. E. Gomes, & A. D.Kramer (Eds.), *Ecopsychology: Restoring the earth, Healing the Mind* (pp. 1–17). San Francisco: Sierra Club Books.

Sanford, J. A. (1995). *Fate, Love and Ecstasy: Wisdom From the Lesser Known Goddesses of the Greeks.* Wilmette, IL: Chiron.

Stroud, J. H. (1996). "Aphrodite and the Ensouled World." In J. H. Stroud (Ed.), *The Olympians: Ancient Deities as Archetypes* (pp. 104–116). New York: Continuum.

Walker, B. (1988). *The Woman's Dictionary of Symbols and Sacred Objects.* San Francisco: Harper & Row.

---

[3] From *Cypria*, as quoted by Athenaeus, Deipnosophistai, 15.682 d-f, trans. Evelyn-White, Hugh G. 1967, p. 499.

2) APOLLO
Apollo Updated:
Zero Effect

(Note: This essay was originally published in The San Francisco Jung Institute Library Journal, November 2000, Volume 19, Number 3, Pages 71-79.)

When I was eight, I couldn't get enough of the famous Sherlock Holmes detective mysteries by Sir Arthur Conan Doyle. My love for the clever fictional sleuth has never died. I was elated when, in March 1997, I first heard about the independent movie *Zero Effect*. I couldn't wait to see it because of young writer/director Jake Kasdan's hip, updated twist on Holmes and Watson; I loved the film the first time I saw it. But it wasn't until a recent second viewing, as the film made its cable/rental rounds, that I became aware of its enormous archetypal appeal: the presence of Apollo is the veritable centerpiece of the film.

C. G. Jung, in a lecture delivered to the Society of German Language and Literature in Zürich, 1922, said:

> The impact of an archetype, whether it takes the form of immediate experience or is expressed through the spoken word, stirs us because it summons up a voice that is stronger than our own. (C.G. Jung. *The Spirit in Man, Art*

and Literature, translated by R.F.C. Hull. Bollingen Series XX, Princeton UP, 1966, p. 82)

I had been stirred up by Kasdan's modern re-visioning of Apollo. But what does a contemporary update of Apollo have to offer us, in a time when many feel there is too much Apollonian energy in our culture, too many detached, narrowly-focused individuals who are unable to truly connect? The complex mytheme of Apollo does have a healing effect, especially when realized with all its lights and shadows, as in *Zero Effect*.

The plot evolves around Daryl Zero (played by Bill Pullman) who is the world's "most private" and brilliant detective. Zero's methodology of deduction is "the two Obs," objectivity and observation. The reclusive gumshoe lives alone in a high tower above an unnamed city, only venturing out in public to solve a crime when he must, and often in disguise. His well-heeled lawyer/assistant Steve Arlo (portrayed by Ben Stiller) functions as his intermediary to the "real world." The film begins with Arlo's meeting with an important millionaire named Stark (Ryan O'Neal) in Portland, Oregon. Stark has a blackmail problem he wishes Zero to solve.

Act One, Scene One: The Mysterious Daryl Zero

This initial segment establishes private detective Daryl Zero as isolated; he has no direct communication with anyone other than his sidekick. Millionaire Stark comments that it is all very unusual and wonders where Zero resides; Arlo refuses to say. These elements evoke the image of Apollo, as Christine Downing notes:

> Still, most of us, I imagine, first think of Apollo as the god to whom [Walter] Otto introduces us in his beautiful portrait: mysterious and unapproachable, calm and lofty, a god who comes from afar and withdraws for part of

each year to a remote, mysterious place. (Christine Downing. *Gods in Our Midst*. New York, Crossroad, 1993, p. 85)

Apollo's energy as constellated in Zero is further enhanced by Zero's ties to music; we hear him play and sing an original song on the guitar for two minutes after the initial scene. Arlo identifies Zero as a musician and songwriter. This, too, is part of Apollo's archetype. "It was as the god of music and poetry that Apollo was portrayed on Mount Parnassus"; Apollo's instrument is the lyre. (Pierre Grimal. *The Dictionary of Classical Mythology*. Blackwell, 1996, p. 50)

Arlo adds to Zero's Apollonian mystique when he tells Stark that the detective has "a deeply nuanced and thoroughly functional understanding of human behavior to rival the great psychoanalytical minds of our times." Here Arlo implies that Zero has omnipotent powers based on his super-reasoning ability; Zero didn't even leave home to solve "The Case of The Man With the Mismatched Shoelaces," a crime which stymied "the Feds" but which Zero solved in an hour of desk work. As Ginette Paris says: "We certainly need the rationality and formal rigor of Apollo..." (Ginette Paris. *Pagan Meditations*, translated by Gwendolyn Moore. Woodstock, CT, Spring Publications, 1997, p. 17)

Zero's Loft, Bolted Entries, Golden Streaks, Laurels

Eight minutes into the film, we're introduced to a modern high-rise in which Zero occupies the top floor, the penthouse. Arlo must use a complicated series of keys and security code clearances in order to gain entry to Zero's domicile. Filmmaker Kasdan devotes substantial time to this event—about a minute. It brings to mind part of Callimachus's *Hymn to Apollo*:

> Bolts of the doors, thrust yourselves back.
> Keys—open the doors! For the god is no longer far away.
> "So, young men, prepare yourself for singing and dancing."
> (qtd. in Karl Kerényi. *Apollo*, Jon Solomon, trans. Dallas: Spring Publications, 1983, p. 20)

Zero's music accompanies the door-opening ritual, leading to shots of guitar strings—which evoke imagistic links to Apollo's stringed lyre. The camera angles down a labyrinth of dark hallways until finally, in the light, the striking Bill Pullman as Zero is seen standing on a bed, with sun-streaked hair and a shirt with green leaf imprints, reminiscent of laurel leaves. These elements, too, echo Callimachus's descriptions:

> "Golden is Apollo's mantle and golden is its clasp
> As are his lyre…"
> (qtd. in Kerényi, p. 24)

Apollo's identification with the sun, or as "the solar god," is embodied by the actor here. (Paris, p. 19) As for laurels, Grimal notes in his *Dictionary of Classical Mythology*: "The bay laurel was the plant of Apollo above all others. It was a bay leaf that the Pythia chewed during her prophetic trances." (p. 50) Thus, the first full shot of Zero gives us a modern incarnation of Apollo.

Love Life
There is homoerotic tension in the relationship between Zero and Arlo that remains outside direct discussion, although embodied in subtext throughout the film; we see the beginnings of it at this early point in Act One. When alone with Arlo in his home or in hotels, Zero flirts. Zero's most vulnerable scenes are with Arlo, and there are many discussions defining the nature of their business

relationships. In all the Zero-Arlo scenes, Zero's hair is blonder, even permed; and all these segments are set in interior bedroom locales.

Both Zero and Apollo are "attended by males" (Downing, p. 86); Arlo is Zero's sole attendant. Downing cites Robert Eisner's observation that "Apollo's homosexuality is really a sterile narcissism: in others he loves only his own traits." (Downing, p. 86) We see that realized throughout the film.

Yet Apollo tries to woo women. "He [Apollo] is a lover of women, too...but they, evidently not experiencing his love as love, refuse him as a lover." (*Idem*) Part of *Zero Effect*'s progression involves a failed attempt at romance between Zero and a character named Gloria Sullivan, portrayed by Kim Dickens. We learn in the opening sequence that, according to sidekick Arlo, Zero has never even kissed a girl. From his lofty office in the sky, Zero, like Apollo, regards "women *from above*" (Paris, p. 19), which is part of the reason he is unable to become truly involved in a romance.

Apollonian Think Tank

Zero accepts Stark's blackmail case, and deduces that there are twenty-four hours to solve it, due to the blackmailer's most recent demand for money. In a scene near the end of Act One, as the plot progresses, we get a sense of Zero's omnipotence; his massive walls of computers serve as a symbol for the giant human brain. From his secret station in the clouds, Zero is able to book an airline ticket for Arlo in ten seconds, sending his assistant/sidekick back to Portland. Zero is the unseen master controller, at the nexus of all activity—a metaphoric reference to the sun:

> For the Greeks, Apollo was something quite special, more than son of the celestial body, and even more than the mature paternal sun God. Like all the great

Olympians, he is, so to speak, the center of the world from which the whole of existence seems to have a different appearance.

(Kerényi, pages 44-45)

The Two "Obs," The Sun Circles, The Image of Zero

Zero explains his disciplined methodology in a hilarious segment in Act Two, and chronicles it himself on his computer, since Arlo refuses to transcribe it for him. In Zero's documentation of his own methods, he demonstrates his use of "The Two Obs: Objectivity and Observation." Zero's mental practice highlights that "Apollo is intellect, discipline purity." (Vincent Scully, *The Earth, The Temple and the Gods*, New Haven, Yale UP, 1979, p. 100) Zero emphasizes his own aloofness with the line: "I have mastered the fine art of detachment." Walter Otto notes of the god: "Apollo rejects whatever is too near." (Walter Otto, *Dionysus: Myth and Culture*, Bloomington, IN: Indiana UP, 1965, p. 78) Zero specifies "supreme objectivity" as a great strength. This is key to Apollo's archetypal presence: "Apollo represents clarity, coolness, objectivity…" (Downing, p. 85)

In Act Two, there is an aerial shot of Zero in his think tank. The computers surround him, fanning out like sunbeams, with Zero in the center of the oval. Later, as Zero discusses the art of research, we see him curled up in a window shaped like an orb; filmmaker Kasdan literally has Zero inhabit the sun here, high above the darkened room. There, Zero embodies the Apollonian "bright and dark, transparent but also abundant in dangers and misfortunes, the source of which is the 'spirit.'" (Kerényi, p. 45)

It is important to reflect on Kasdan's choice of the character name "Zero"; this image constellates Apollonian imagery. "Zero" brings to mind myriad symbols: 0 as a numeric starting/ending point; a circle, an orb; infinity; the sound "O"—the same ending as the word "Apollo"; nothingness. There is an association of nihilism with zero. This, too, connects to the god:

> "Apollo is, as seen from the viewpoint of the soul, an aspect of the individual's ceasing to be, of a reality which when seen from one angle is dark...This is Apollo, the soul's darkness and the soul's clarity." (Kerényi, p. 58)

Kasdan highlights this association physically in this Act Two scene, with Zero reading in the orb-shaped window.

Zero's Beauty, Birds

Zero's handsome looks are, of course, part of the archetypal incarnation. Mary E. Barnard writes: "...Apollo, the brightest god of the Olympian pantheon. He has beauty, grace..." (Mary E. Barnard, *The Myth of Apollo and Daphne from Ovid to Quevedo: Love, Agon and the Grotesque*. Durham, NC: Duke UP, 1987, p. 3) Callimachus describes Apollo as "Always fair, always young!" (qtd. in Kerényi, p. 24); he personifies manly beauty. Although Zero appears in disguise during much of the movie, he is often strikingly handsome, as in an Act Two close-up shot where Zero discovers the importance of birds to the blackmail mystery.

Although there are no swans in the film, birds become a major focus of the Stark case. In another scene in Act Two, we are introduced to a strange poem about "Plummeting Birds," a topic which recurs three additional times during the film. Interestingly, there are no actual visuals of birds but repeated allusions to them in dialogue and metaphoric imagery. The kite, the vulture, and the crow are attributed to Apollo. (Grimal, p. 50) We later learn that the poetic bird references that Zero uncovers were created by a murderer. In the killer's poem, the birds are swooping, falling, "plummeting"; these connotations color the bird allusions as dark and sinister, like the birds of prey listed above. This is another manifestation of the "dark" side of Apollo's world. Kerényi notes that ravens and crows were key to Apollo's myth: "The dark birds...represent his essence just as does the swan in his other aspect." (Kerényi, p. 56)

Expert Marksman; Killer Side

Apollo had, as Callimachus notes, a "Lyctian bow and quiver" (qtd. in Kerényi, p. 24) and was famous for "the strength of an unerring marksman." (Barnard, p. 3) He also had a great skill—renowned deadly aim, as Downing indicates: "It may be strange at first to think of Apollo as a murderer, as a killer. But what is central here is the possibility of purification, the possibility...of putting an end to seemingly endless cycles of blood vengeance." (Downing, p. 89) Thus, the "killer side" of Apollo is connected to the notion of purification that the archetype embodies. Kasdan begins to foreshadow Zero's purifying powers related to "the killer" in Apollo near the end of Act Two, although Zero never literally kills. Zero has one social encounter in the film with Gloria Sullivan, a woman he meets in a gym and whom he suspects is part of the scheme. Gloria's idea of a fun date is target practice with guns and rifles; Zero pretends not to be able to shoot when they go to a remote area for some firing practice one night after dinner. There is a discussion of "aim"; he misses the target the first time, and takes a long time to set up his next shot. When he thinks Gloria is not looking, Zero reveals his expert marksmanship and hits the target like a pro.

Objectivity Reiterated; Zero as Purifier, Healer

"Passion is the enemy of precision" says Zero, as he describes why his lack of passion allows him to observe what others, in the throes of passion, do. Kasdan reiterates Zero's detachment in Act Three, near the climax of the film, and affirms Zero's "archetypal premise in Apollo, where detachment, dispassion, exclusive masculinity, clarity, formal beauty, farsighted aim, and elitism" shape his destiny. (James Hillman. *Re-Visioning Psychology*. HarperPerennial, 1975, p. 132)

In the climax of this film, Zero solves the mystery, revealing that Gloria, the blackmailer of Stark, is really Stark's daughter from a rape that occurred decades ago. Stark, author of the "Plummeting Birds" poem, ordered the murder of Gloria's mother, Clarissa; when the hit man realized that a baby witnessed the killing, he opted to save baby Gloria without revealing the child's existence to Stark. Thus, the mystery is solved. "The bringing of harmony into the boundless confusion, the discovery of order in chaos, are both Apollo's gifts." (Arianna Huffington. *The Gods of Greece*. New York: Atlantic Monthly Press, 1993, p. 45)

But Zero, as purifier/healer, does not reveal all of this information to the murderous Stark; instead, he allows Gloria Sullivan-Stark to leave town undetected, to escape, to be free. Here Zero, like Apollo, puts an end to "endless cycles of blood vengeance…For a god to have to power to free us from this fear is to be a god indeed." (Downing, p. 89) This is an important characteristic of the archetype, as Apollo was the god of healing and ceremonial purification. Alone at his computer think tank, after returning from Portland, Zero dubs the Stark episode "The Case of the Man Who Got So Stressed Out Over His Lost Keys That He Eventually Had A Heart Attack and It Turns Out They Were In His Sofa All Along." Zero highlights the importance of "Observation and Intervention" in his work, and he officially names his sleuthing process "The Zero Effect." Zero, in Apollonian fashion, has made the separate pieces of the case fit together so they are part of a whole. "…Apollo holds all together in harmony." (Kerényi, p. 55)

In the final shot of *Zero Effect*, after solving the case, a solitary Zero composes his story in his secure, secret sky-top domicile, surrounded by his sun-spiraling computer bay, seated in the center of his circular set-up, wearing his green, laurel-leafed shirt again. At the end, right before the screen finally fades to black, when Zero is lit up by the glow of the computer screens, it is the visage of the god we see, the face of Apollo. Then Kasdan gives us: Blackout. Back to zero.

According to Jung, *archetypal activation* is the secret of all great art.

"The creative process, so far as we are able to follow it all, consists in the unconscious activation of an archetypal image, and in elaborating and shaping this image into the finished work. By giving it shape, the artist translates it into the language of the present, and so makes it possible for us to find our way back to the deepest springs of life. Therein lies the social significance of art: it is constantly at work educating the spirit of the age, conjuring up the forms in which the age is most lacking." (C.G. Jung, p. 82)

Our age lacks true archetypal representation of Apollo's dualistic nature. The dynamic tension between the opposites inherent in the Apollonian mytheme are rarely examined in our current culture; filmmaker Kasdan bravely celebrates them in *Zero Effect*. Too often in modern movies, we have reductive, partial Apollonian reflections which highlight only the god's reasoning powers; specific mythological binarisms are ignored.

For Apollo is both light and dark, deliberately detached and desperately longing for attachment, incisively brainy and romantically clueless, physically beautiful yet still repellant, healer and killer, with the ability to transform others with his considerable talents, yet with a pronounced inability to change himself. Apollo is the nexus who cannot connect.

Kasdan give us Apollo's dark pain, the god's ironic downside—something that is not often addressed yet it is of primary psychic importance. Our dot.com culture prizes connection, but in the service of commerce and information, not soul. This is the healing function of an updated Apollo: to remind us of the hazards of electronic elitism, because there is a high price to pay. With a click of a mouse, Apollo can solve a problem from a distance; yet, ultimately, he is lonely, ostracized by his own impotence—an inability to relate. Thus, Apollo's mytheme is dangerous, cautionary, purifying, restorative—and timely. "Thus, just as one-sidedness of the individual's conscious attitude is corrected by reactions from the unconscious, so art represents a process of self-regulation in the life of nations and epochs." (C.G. Jung, p. 83)

Works Cited

Barnard, Mary E. *The Myth of Apollo and Daphne from Ovid to Quevedo: Love, Agon and the Grotesque.* Durham, NC: Duke UP, 1987.

Downing, Christine. *Gods In Our Midst.* New York: Crossroad, 1993.

Grimal, Pierre. *The Dictionary of Classical Mythology.* N.p.: Blackwell, 1996.

Hillman, James. *Re-Visioning Psychology.* N.p.: HarperPerennial, 1975.

Huffington, Arianna. *The Gods of Greece.* New York: Atlantic Monthly Press, 1993.

Jung, C.G. *The Spirit in Man, Art and Literature.* Trans. R.F.C. Hull. Bollingen Series XX, Princeton UP, 1966.

Kerényi, Karl. *Apollo.* Trans. Jon Solomon. Dallas: Spring Publications, 1983.

Otto, Walter F. *Dionysus: Myth and Cult*. Bloomington: Indiana UP, 1965.

Paris, Ginette. *Pagan Meditations*. Trans. Gwendolyn Moore. Woodstock, CT: Spring Publications, 1997.

Scully, Vincent. *The Earth, The Temple, and the Gods*. New Haven, Yale UP, 1979.

Zero Effect. Dir. Jake Kasdan. Screenplay by Jake Kasdan. Perf. Bill Pullman, Ben Stiller, Kim Dickens, Ryan O'Neal. 1997. Videocassette. Castle Rock Entertainment, 1998.

3) ARTEMIS
Unseen Beauty:
Artemis and Dark Matter

(Note: "Unseen Beauty: Artemis and Dark Matter" was originally published in Mythopoetry Scholar, Volume 2, "Matter and Beauty." Mythopoetry.com, January 2, 2011. It was published with a photo I took of "Diane de Versailles" in the Louvre, Paris, April 2010.)

"And when she [Artemis] has hung up this unstrung bow,
When she has put away her arrows,
She puts on, over her flesh, a beautiful dress..."
    —"The Second Hymn to Artemis," *The Homeric Hymns*[4]

Paradoxical connections between beauty and dark matter in the universe may be explored through stories and characteristics of the archetype Artemis.

Although Aphrodite is often heralded as the most attractive deity in the Greek pantheon, the goddess Artemis is noted for her youthful, virginal beauty. Popular Artemis,[5] twin sister to Apollo, is known as "Diana" in Roman myth. She's the "nature girl" archetype, Mistress of the Animals, equally at home roaming meadows, mountains, or forests. The deer and the bear are sacred to her. She's tall, slim, athletic, and lovely. But Artemis is also *"potnia semnotata*—mistress most terrible and holy" (Gregory 64). She hunts to kill, and carries her quiver of arrows everywhere. The god Pan gave her a pack of hunting dogs; she usually brings along seven hounds on the hunt. Artemis is the patron goddess of the Amazons, and is often accompanied by nymphs. As a goddess, she presides over the act of birth, and sometimes imposes pain on women who die in childbirth (Grimal 61). "To understand Artemis' divine image we need to somehow see that grace and loveliness most rendered by the poets, together with the awesomeness revealed in her cults of worship" (Gregory 64), which entailed "intensity, darkness, and even savagery" (Gregory 65).[6] Artemis is associated with the moon, "her silver bow a glistening symbol of the lunar crescent" (Andrews 17). Artemis/Diana travels "through the night in a silver chariot drawn by white horses and shot moonbeams through the sky with her silver bow" (Andrews 17). Her evening beauty is illuminated in the darkness of the night sky.

The beauty of the heavens—distant stars and galaxies—have long fascinated humankind. We name key stars for gods and goddesses, emblematic of our admiration and celestial aspirations. Even in the twenty-first century, standards of beauty are still colloquially expressed in astronomical terms: "She lights up the room—a true star." Movie and television "stars" are international icons of physical perfection.

Scientific research suggests that mysterious dark matter—unseen but evidenced by gravitational pull—occupies the universe like "a sea of invisible particles that fills space unevenly" (Feng and Trodden 40). NASA scientists estimate that dark matter inhabits about twenty-five percent of the universe ("Dark Energy"). Historically, scientists have not always been aware of the presence of dark matter, although it is suggested that galaxies and galaxy clusters are haloed with it ("Dark Matter"). Astrophysicists are puzzled by what dark matter is and what it does. "For such a mass of material to elude detection, astronomers reason that it has to consist of particles that scarcely interact with ordinary matter or, indeed, with each other. All they do is provide the platform for luminous matter" (Feng and Trodden 40). Perhaps dark matter is the invisible scaffolding underpinning ordinary matter: if that is so, you cannot see light without the unheralded and difficult-to-observe presence of dark matter.

In "Dark Worlds," from the November 2010 *Scientific American*, physicists Jonathan Feng and Mark Trodden explain one theory which suggests that "dark matter may be accompanied by a hidden weak force or, even more remarkably, a hidden version of electromagnetism, implying that dark matter may emit and reflect hidden light" (45).

One iconic image of the goddess Artemis is that of "Artemis Phosophorus" or the "torch-bearing Artemis" (Sourvinou-Inwood 183) or "light-bringer."

Ginette Paris writes of Artemis: "The myth even makes her a Goddess whose beauty should not be exposed to human sight, as if to signify that this beauty exists for itself. The myths associated with Artemis suggest that one may hear her or sense her presence, but that it is dangerous to violate her, even with the eyes" (114). Artemis demands that her beauty not be contemplated by mortals nor reflected in mirroring waters. It is not a beauty to be shared.

Two tales of Artemis are relevant to the exploration of connections between aspects of beauty and properties of dark matter. The first story involves the hunter Actaeon. One day, Artemis was bathing in a pure spring, secluded in the forest with her nymphs. Actaeon, hunting in the woods with his fifty hounds, came upon the ravishing goddess and her enchanting female entourage. He hid, watching them as they bathed, but Artemis discovered him. Angrily, she turned the hunter into a stag, and then set his fifty hounds loose upon him. Since Artemis had transformed him into a deer, the dogs didn't recognize their master. They ate him: "...then hunted for him in vain throughout the forest, which echoed with their howls" (Grimal 10).

The second story involves the river god Alpheus, who was enamored with Artemis. Frustrated that he could not have her through "proper channels," Alpheus schemed to kidnap the wild nature goddess. At a festival at Letrenoi, Alpheus went to see Artemis. But she got wind of his plans, and disguised herself. Artemis covered her visage with mud and was able to escape undetected—as Alpheus didn't recognize the deity in her mask (Grimal 35).

In the myth of Artemis and Actaeon, the hunter is killed after witnessing the goddess and her beauty mirrored in the spring; in the second story, Artemis's beauty is masked by the hands of the goddess herself and thus remains undiscovered. Like dark matter in the universe—existing but unseen, hidden yet revealed synecdochically by its density—Artemis insists that her loveliness remain a celestial secret: her extraordinary beauty seemingly known only to the gods, or perhaps the Amazons. Beauty is best, in Artemisian terms, if it is unsung, unseen, unknown, and self-avenged if transgressed (e.g. the goddess will hunt the beauty-seeker). Gregory, in her essay "Artemis," says that the deity is "bewildering" in the true sense of the word, in that the goddess leads us to the wild, the unknown, the undefined, "as opposed to the civilized" (66).

The sphere of Artemis's beauty is paradoxical. It's there, but you can't see it. Hidden, it lights up the universe, the heavens. The search for proof of dark matter in the universe is also paradoxical. "How to see the unseeable…So far everything astronomers know about dark matter comes from its gravitational effects on visible matter. But they need to detect it directly if they are to find out what it is. That will not be easy: dark matter is elusive by definition. Nevertheless…thousands of researchers are looking" (Feng and Trodden 44).

As Artemis will hunt and kill the beauty seeker, thus defining an aspect of self-protection and retaliation directly related to her pulchritude, so dark matter has a relationship with destruction. Through the "titanic collision" of galaxy clusters, dark matter may become separated from ordinary matter; images of this have been captured by the Hubble Space Telescope ("Dark Energy").

Through the lens of astronomy and the search for dark matter, the aesthetics of Artemis's beauty may be explored in fresh ways. Parallels and paradoxes in the myths of Artemis and the celestial search for dark matter point to a heavenly beauty that eludes observation; an invisible force (and perhaps an aesthetic) true to itself, that defies current categories of function and purpose; a gravity that reveals its significance, as it emits hidden light which defies reflection; a prettiness that can evoke destruction; a pure loveliness that exists beyond our comprehension and imaginations; and whose anomalies are mere glimmers of shimmering worlds we cannot know.

> "She [Artemis] puts on, over her flesh, a beautiful dress...
> Then she begins the dances and their sound is heavenly."
> –"The Second Hymn to Artemis," *The Homeric Hymns*

Works Cited

Andrews, Tamra. *A Dictionary of Nature Myths: Legends of the Earth, Sea and Sky*. Oxford: Oxford UP, 1998.

"Artemis." "Greek Gods" phone application. Godchecker.com. 14 December 2010.

"Dark Energy, Dark Matter." NASA Science. 4 January 2011. http://science.nasa.gov/astrophysics/focus-areas/what-is-dark-energy/.

"Dark Matter." Wikipedia. 15 December 2010.
http://en.wikipedia.org/wiki/Dark_matter.

Feng, Jonathan and Mark Trodden. "Dark Worlds: A Shadow Cosmos In Our Midst May Be as Dynamic as the Visible One." *Scientific American*, November 2010, Volume 303, Number 5. 38-45.

Grimal, Pierre. *The Dictionary of Classical Mythology*. Trans. by A.R. Maxwell-Hyslop. Oxford: Blackwell, 1996.

Gregory, Eileen. "Artemis." *The Olympians: Ancient Deities as Archetypes*. Joanne H. Stroud, Ed. New York: Continuum, 1996. 64-75.

The Homeric Hymns, Charles Boer, trans. Woodstock, CT: Spring Publications, 1970.

Paris, Ginette. *Pagan Mediations: Aphrodite, Hestia, Artemis*. Gwendolyn Moore, trans. Woodstock, CT: Spring Publications, 1997.

Sourvinou-Inwood, Christiane. "Artemis." *The Oxford Classical Dictionary*. Hornblower, Simon and Anthony Spawforth, eds. Third Edition. Oxford: Oxford University Press, 2003. 182-184.

---

[4] "The Second Hymn to Artemis," *The Homeric Hymns*. 5.

[5] According to their "Greek Gods" smart phone application [2011], Artemis is "by far the most requested deity at Godchecker.com."

[6] "At Patrae the festival Laphria included a procession in which a virgin priestess rode in a chariot drawn by deer and the holocaust sacrifice of many animals; these were thrown alive into the altar enclosure, and included wild animals such as deer and boar, which were not normally sacrificed in Greek religion" (Sourvino-Inwood 184). Human sacrifice was also part of her cult rituals, such as at Tauris (Grimal 62).

4) ATHENA
Pieces of Athena (and Her Head)

(Note: This essay is published for the first time in this volume.)

It's April 21, 2004. I'm giving an informal luncheon talk as part of the Center for Feminist Research's Affiliated Scholar activities at the University of Southern California, in Los Angeles. I have chosen the topic of "female mentors in current film" as my general subject, and I start with a definition of the term "mentor." I distribute a handout about Homer, *The Odyssey,* and Athena, who, in disguise as Mentor, guided Telemachus. I discuss the term "mentor," and relate it to the female mentor figures I observe in the films "The Matrix," "Legally Blonde 2," "Mona Lisa Smile," the "Harry Potter" series, "Minority Report," and "Cold Mountain." I end by mentioning key characters from "Whale Rider," "Pieces of April," and "Finding Nemo." I conclude: "I have highlighted several examples of the female mentor: 1) the warrior-mentor, 2) the betrayer-mentor, 3) the young teacher and the old teacher, and the young heroine-culture healer." But after the talk, I wonder if I've really shed any light on the subject of the female mentor at all. Maybe I've shed light on the images of female mentors in current popular cinema or lack thereof? I end my talk with questions, such as: "Why isn't the archetypal role of 'the female mentor' more prevalent in pop culture and entertainment?"

I am on a journey to try to understand Athena more deeply; what is her function as a mentor? I can give you only snippets (like fast-loading photo files on a Flickr page), and they are sometimes out of order.

It's March 10, 2011. I'm at home in Los Angeles on the computer reading about the modern usage of "mentor" on Wikipedia.org. François Fénelon's *Les Aventures de Télémaque*, created in 1699, features Mentor as the protagonist. The book centers on a teacher-pupil relationship, detailing Telemachus' relationship with Mentor, trusted friend of Odysseus; Fénelon's satire of Louis XIV's reign was popular during the 1700's and became a bestseller, leading to our use of the word "mentor" today.[7] As a punishment for penning this satire (and for other issues), Louis XIV banished Fénelon from Versailles; he lived in a sort of cultural exile in his diocese.[8] *Les Aventures de Télémaque* was an inspiration to Jean-Jacques Rousseau who penned *Émile ou de l'education* in 1762.[9] Goddess Minerva (the Roman version of Athena) protects Telemachus with divine guidance throughout the work.

It is October 1, 2010, and I'm in New York at the Metropolitan Museum of Art. I am downstairs in the fantastic Greek and Roman Art section. I love this collection. I stand in front of a "colossal" marble head of Athena, but there is no helmet. It looks as if it has been lopped off, along with the rest of her body. Her head is somewhat chopped at the top, where the helmet would have been. Her turning face is supposed to represent the warrior in motion, according to curatorial information. I try to imagine the rest of her there, on the way to defend or protect something. With only her face and neck on the pedestal, it becomes an exercise in synecdoche. I snap pictures from three different angles.

It's July 24, 2006, and I'm at the Getty Villa in Malibu, California, taking photos of statues of mythological figures in their collection. It's crowded and hot. I am especially fascinated with "The Helmeted Head of Athena" by Artist Unknown, thought to be a part of a statue from Pergamon, circa 160-150 C.E.[10] This statue has been completely dismembered; only Athena's head remains. Lonely, the stone orb sits atop a pedestal. Her nose is cut off. Her lip is split. It is metaphoric, I think, that we find Athena so fragmented here. This statue must have been powerfully iconic at one time, yet she seems so disembodied now. Someone deliberately defaced her, too, or so it appears. There is a mere sliver of her helmet still remaining on her head—a shadowy decorative band to signal her legendary intellectual, strategic prowess. Even so, she looks beautiful. I try to imagine the full helmet on the statue's head, because today it looks more like a diadem. I take a profile shot of Athena's head; you can see the helmet design a bit better from the side, and the gash to her lip is less noticeable. Unfortunately, I capture the green "Exit" sign in the top left of the photo. I don't want to crop it out, though, because I really like the lines of her profile. She was born of Zeus' head, and her head is all that remains here. The statue was most likely made in Pergamon (what is now Turkey) as a classical imitation of a statue from Athens.[11] The information plaque says the statue was repaired around the head even "in antiquity"; the drill holes around the top of her forehead are quite visible, in profile. Thus, care for this Athena's head is not only a modern event; her head was tended in antiquity, too. The guide notes also say that from the current angle of her head, one can deduce that Athena's body was most likely turned to the left. I leave the statue, thinking about the holes in it—holes for her helmet, her battle scars.

It's late December 2002. I'm at home in Los Angeles. I'm reading *The Eumenides*, the final play in Aeschylus' *The Orestia*, trying to determine if I will assign the play in my new critical studies class "The Archetypal Feminine: From the Greeks to Contemporary Drama," which starts in January 2003. Orestes, who killed Clytemnestra, clings to Athena's statue in front of her temple, seeking spiritual sanctuary. This arouses the anger of The Furies, who intend to avenge Clytemnestra's death.[12] When "Pallas Athena" enters and is confronted with this, she says to Orestes:

> "O man unknown, make thou thy plea in turn.
> Speak forth thy land, thy lineage, and thy woes;
> Then, if thou canst, avert this bitter blame
> If, as I deem, in confidence of right
> Thou sittest hard beside my holy place,
> Clasping this statue, as Ixion sat,
> A sacred suppliant for Zeus to cleanse,
> To all this answer me in words made plain."[13]

In this play, a statue of Athena is important. Athena assembles a jury for the first ever murder trial. Apollo testifies on behalf of Orestes, and in effect functions as his counselor; Orestes had sought purification at Apollo's temple. Of the trial's outcome, Athena says:

> "Mine is the right to add the final vote,
> And I award it to Orestes' cause.
> For me no mother bore within her womb,
> And, save for wedlock evermore eschewed,
> I vouch myself the champion of the man,

> Not of the woman, yea, with all my soul,
> In heart, as birth, a father's child alone.
> Thus will I not too heinously regard
> A woman's death who did her husband slay,
> The guardian of her home; and if the votes
> Equal do fall, Orestes shall prevail."[14]

Athena sides with the men, citing her famous birth story (in which she was born from Zeus' head) as foundational to her perspective—a connection to the "justice" function of the Zeus archetype. The Furies are enraged by Orestes' acquittal. But Athena negotiates: she assuages them, offers sanctuary, and instructs Athenians to respect them as sacred goddesses. The play ends with a procession of Athenian women and children escorting *The Eumenides* ("the gracious ones," as they are now renamed) back to their caves. The final lines are: "All-seeing Zeus and Fate come down/To battle fair for Pallas' town! Ring out your chant, ring out your joy's acclaim!"[15] Seemingly, Athena brings about a happy ending. Is Athena a mentor to the Furies? She has brought peace to the polis. I decide not to assign the play in January; I don't understand Athena well enough yet.

It's mid-May 2010 and I'm in Los Angeles at home. Soon I will teach a Goddess Workshop for women playwrights at the Los Angeles Women's Theatre Project. I'm thinking again about the meaning of "mentor" as I expect to speak about Athena as a figure of inspiration (and other goddesses, too) in this workshop of all women participants. I realize, in a panic, that I have not spent enough time considering if/how Athena is an inspirational mentor figure as related to women. I know she helped Telemachus; I know why she sides with Orestes in *The Eumenides*. In her 2008 book

Athena, Susan Deacy writes that Athena is, among other things, "a goddess of women's work"[16] related to craft and the domestic arts.[17] Ariadne comes to mind. In "Theseus and Athenian Festivals" Erika Simon notes: "Artists from the earlier fifth century on combine Athena also with a dark point in Theseus' life, the abandoning of Ariadne."[18] Deacy states of Athena: "women of myth often come to grief when they come into contact with her."[19] In addition to Ariadne, Deacy lists others: Arachne, who is changed into a spider after challenging Athena in a weaving contest; Murmix who, upon clashing with Athena over the creation of the plough, was turned into an ant; beautiful Medusa,[20] who was changed into ugliness after having sex in Athena's temple with Poisedon; and Pallas, daughter of river god Triton, who was accidentally killed by Athena in a childhood incident.[21] Carefully, I build a slide for Athena in my PowerPoint presentation; as an image, I use a photo of the "Athena Mattei," whom I've seen before.

It's the end of April 2010. I'm in Paris at the Louvre, in the Greek, Etruscan and Roman Antiquities section. It is crowded; tomorrow is a national labor holiday so everyone is here, the atmosphere is festive, and the museum is open late. I'm staring at the "Athena Mattei" statue. I'm glad to see Athena's head on this statue, because the magnificent "Ingres Minerva" in this same museum doesn't have one. I am struck by the distinctive nature of her ribbony "Gorgon" warrior-goddess aegis: Medusa's little head on Athena's snaky sash, Perseus' gift, a weapon. Left hand outstretched. Right hand on hip. Helmet on head. Not smiling. Yet not grim either. This is a Roman copy of a Greek statue, the Piraeus Athena, but not an exact one. It is an "adaptation." She is also called "Athena Pacifique," or peaceful Athena.[22] Some feel this stance is welcoming, and the outstretched arm a greeting. To me, it looks like she's saying: "On the other hand..." It is so refreshing to see a head connected to the body of her statue: you get a sense of her great power when she's all in one piece.

It is May 18, 2011, and I'm in Bath, England, at the Roman Baths.[23] I am dripping wet. It is raining, humid, and the halls are crowded with tourists. The complex is filled with energetic young French students on a field trip. They have some sort of intensive school project to complete that involves sketching the exhibits' highlights. It is difficult to get a good look at all the displays, but I try to squeeze in to take photos whenever there's a break in the queues. I am grateful to be here in mid-May, before the height of the summer season; it will become more crowded in June, July and August. This is my fourth time to the Roman Baths, but it's been twenty years since I last visited. The exhibition has changed a great deal since my last tour so many years ago; it's completely modernized. There are now film projections and computerized displays. I climb up to the seventh row in the small informal amphitheatre and watch the animated presentation about one of the more famous objects here, rediscovered in a dig in 1790: The Gorgon's Head.[24] This is a little show, a sort of ten-minute indoor *son et lumière*, and the beautiful features of this centerpiece are illuminated with lighting changes, including colors and shapes. There is a bit of mystery, too. Experts debate if the centerpiece is truly a Gorgon's Head or not; it could be Oceanus or a Celtic sun god. It looks more male than female. There is also a statuette of a perched owl in this same pediment. The owl was sacred to Athena, her primary symbol, and as Deacy writes: "so closely connected...that it might be described as her familiar."[25] As the Gorgon's Head is also a symbol of Athena, I am beginning to feel the presence of the goddess in this sacred spring.

It is still May 18, 2011, one hour later. I'm standing in a dark chamber in front of the famous radiant bronze head of Sulis Minerva. She is unbelievably beautiful, otherworldly, glinting green. She catches your eye as soon as you enter the temple courtyard excavation area from fifty feet away, but the closer you get, she becomes more and more dazzling. Sulis Minerva is a syncretized Celtic-Roman goddess. Minerva is the Roman version of Athena, and Sulis is a local Celtic goddess connected to the sacred thermal springs or the "Aquae Sulis," as the Romans referred to them.[26] The Celts were here first, of course, in B.C.E. and established Sulis as goddess of the thermal waters. The springs gained a healing reputation with a Celtic shrine on site; the Romans arrived in early C.E. The healing/spiritual function of the springs was maintained by the Romans, and hence the worship here of "Sulis Minerva." This statue head was found in 1727, but the body of the statue has never been recovered. The use of bronze on the head signifies that this temple and bath were quite special; bronze gilding was unusual in Roman Britain. The entire original statue must have been large and magnificent. Was it featured in the courtyard? I walk around it, staring as if it were a shining jewel. It is the most remarkable statue head I've ever seen. I can see the telltale holes around the edge of her hairline, the marks of a missing helmet. Yes, this statue head must have worn a helmet once; I know now to look for these marks around Athena's crown, the head wounds. It is thought that this beautiful head was deliberately defaced, most likely hammered at the time of the statue's decapitation—either in an effort to demolish the statue's spiritual power due to the rise of Christianity in 391 C.E. (as demanded by Emperor Theodosius), or due to "barbaric" looting of wealth.[27] Yet amazingly, here she is, still shining.

Sulis Minerva reigned over these sacred thermal waters with different powers than those of Athena. Complex Sulis Minerva was the goddess of healing waters but also of vile curses; Roman prayer requests were made to damn specific individuals, through accusations made about actions of their neighbors and/or friends. Romans sought vengeance through her and wrote their requests for punishment on curse tablets, which still exist. Roman coins were cast into the spring waters with wishes, where her spirit was thought to reside. The curses could be seen as related to the "justice" aspect of Athena's archetype, a way to request vengeance from the goddess. This special temple, in addition to its healing waters, employed a haruspex, a special priest who could read natural omens and make predictions about the future. Therefore, the site had an oracular aspect, too.

The balustraded pathway is full of other people trying to gaze at the bronze of Sulis Minerva up close. Eager French students are trying to sketch her head as quickly as they can. I must move on so others may have their turns. Quickly, I look back at the chipped gilded profile of Sulis Minerva as I edge into the next hall where the curse tablets are displayed. Then, I face forward. I can hear the steaming, misty jade sacred spring waters lapping up ahead of me, the path not yet traveled. I turn back. A last look to take one final photo in this dim, mysterious chamber. Yes, her face is potted, and missing pieces, but there is something—sudden shadow play, grey movement near her crown. And I swear for an instant I can see a tall dark helmet in silhouette, perched on her head, as it should be. But when I move my camera up to snap the shot, it is gone.

---

[7] Roberts, Andy. (1999) "The origins of the term mentor," *History of Education Society Bulletin*, No. 64, November 1999, pps. 313–329.
[8] Bell, David A. *The First Total War*. Boston: Mariner, 2007, pps. 58-62.
[9] "*Les Aventures de Télémaque*." Wikipedia.org.
http://en.wikipedia.org/wiki/Les_Aventures_de_Télémaque.

[10] You can see this statue head here: http://www.getty.edu/art/gettyguide/artObjectDetails?artobj=12127.
[11] http://www.getty.edu/art/gettyguide/artObjectDetails?artobj=12127.
[12] Orestes avenged his father with this act: Clytemnestra had plotted against and killed Orestes' father, King Agamemnon.
[13] http://www.sacred-texts.com/cla/aesch/eumend.htm. *The Eumenides* by Aeschylus, trans. Edmund Doidge Anderson Morshead, 1881.
[14] http://www.sacred-texts.com/cla/aesch/eumend.htm. Trans. Morshead.
[15] http://www.sacred-texts.com/cla/aesch/eumend.htm. Trans. Morshead.
[16] Deacy, Susan (2008). *Athena*. London: Routledge. p. 6.
[17] For a related essay, see also "Martha Hearts Hestia" in this collection.
[18] Neils, Jennifer., ed. *Worshipping Athena: Panathenaia and Parthenon*, p. 17.
[19] Deacy, Susan. *Athena*, p. 71.
[20] From "Medusa's Beauty," by Christine de Pizan, trans. Earl Jeffrey Richards. In 1405, in *The Book of the City of Ladies*, de Pizan mentions "ancient stories" about Medusa's legendary beauty. De Pizan writes that Medusa was of "such striking beauty" that she was even "attracted to herself." According to this version, onlookers became immovable because they were overcome by her beauty. "For this reason, the fable claimed they had turned to stone." In *The Medusa Reader*, Marjorie Garber & Nancy J. Vickers, eds. P. 57.
[21] Deacy, Susan. *Athena*, p. 71.
[22] Waywell (G. B.), "Athena Mattei", in *Annual of the British School at Athens*, 66, 1971, pps. 373-382, pl. 66.
[23] http://www.romanbaths.co.uk/, accessed 2 November 2011.
[24] http://www.romanbaths.co.uk/walkthrough/5_temple/the_gorgons_head.aspx.
[25] Deacy, Susan *Athena*, p. 7.
[26] "Sulis Minerva." Wikipedia.org. Accessed 5 February 2012. http://en.wikipedia.org/wiki/Sulis_Minerva.
[27] http://www.romanbaths.co.uk/walkthrough/temple_courtyard.aspx.

5) CASSANDRA
Understanding the Myth:
Why Cassandra Must Not Be Silenced

(Note: This essay was first published in On The Issues Magazine, The Café, *Summer 2011, on July 13, 2011. http://www.ontheissuesmagazine.com)*

The archetype of Cassandra may be seen as a key symbol for women who warn of the dire and immutable consequences of war. The myth of Cassandra—her predictions and the costs of ignoring her—carries an important message for those in anti-war movements, even today.

Cassandra was the female figure in Greek mythology who predicted the Trojan War and its devastation. Cassandra warned of violence connected to the Trojan Horse, and of the ultimate destiny of Paris, who she said would bring about the downfall of Troy. She predicted her father King Priam's negative spiral, foreseeing that he would return with his son Hector's body. Cassandra's predictions were ignored and Troy was ruined. She was branded "treasonous" and mad.

As written by Aeschylus in *Agamemnon*, Cassandra said:

"Alas for the toil, the toil of a City, worn unto death!
Alas for my father's worship before the citadel,
The flocks that bled and the tumult of their breath!
But no help from them came
To save Troy Towers from falling as they fell!...
And I on the earth shall writhe, my heart aflame."

There are several different versions of Cassandra's myth, variations added through time. In most of them, Cassandra has a complicated relationship with the god Apollo, who is credited with giving Cassandra the gift of foresight.

According to one version of her myth, Cassandra was the mortal daughter of King Priam and Queen Hecuba, the royal rulers of Troy (Hunter). The legend held that King Priam had fifty sons and fifty daughters. While she was in Apollo's temple, the god Apollo himself came to visit beautiful Cassandra, and offered her the divine gift of psychic powers. There was only one catch: she had to sleep with him. After Apollo gave Cassandra the ability to prognosticate, she refused to be with him romantically, angering the deity. In revenge, Apollo cursed her: according to his abrasive vow, Cassandra could still predict the future, but no one would ever believe her. She would become an outcast.

In another mythic rendition of her origin, as recounted in Pierre Grimal's *The Dictionary of Classical Mythology*, Cassandra had a twin brother, Helenus. While their parents celebrated the duo's birth (and were not watching the children), two snakes came upon the babes and licked their ears clean. In the morning, the snakes slithered into sacred laurels, a sign of Apollo. Afterward, Cassandra and Helenus had the gift of prophecy (90).

When Apollo, irate and rejected, later sought revenge, he took away Cassandra's confidence in her predictions. Through his curse, she began to doubt her own worth. Although her insights had cultural and spiritual import, no one believed or heeded her. She was marginalized and called "crazy." Her vigorous outcries against patriarchal conventions began to bear consequences; she was isolated. Depressed and alone, Cassandra went "mad." She sought refuge in the Temple of Athena, where she was pursued and attacked by Ajax, even as she held fast to Athena's statue. She was eventually given over to Agamemnon, as part of the spoils of the Trojan War. She died tragically, beheaded by Clytemnestra, who was angry about Agamemnon's betrayal of their marriage.[28]

Cassandra's journey as an anti-war visionary who is ignored and belittled relates to the psychology of anti-war feminists today. When one sees, with certitude, a dark vision for the future, and then is ignored, or worse—dismissed or "cursed" as irrelevant, "anti-patriotic," and powerless—what is the effect on the psyche? Patterns revealed in the Cassandra model suggest that after the shock of disbelief wears away, a numbing ambivalence sets in—a prelude to madness. Jungian analyst Laurie Layton Schapira writes of this tripartite psychological sequence—disbelief, ambivalence, madness—in her 1988 book *The Cassandra Complex: Living With Disbelief*. Schapira concludes with observations about society's damnation of the Cassandra woman who "threaten[s] the conservative order. Thus she speaks treason...we shall continue to attack her for bearing bad tidings. We must be aware, however, that in many cases she bears true witness and neither she, nor we, can any longer afford to disbelieve. The Cassandra woman who escaped the curse of the patriarchal Apollo speaks for a new age" (148).

It is Apollo's revenge on Cassandra that forces the female seer to live in a state of "disbelief"—of not being respected by society or recognized for her anti-war foresight, which could have saved a kingdom. Cassandra's confidence in her own abilities, predictions and talent for intuiting the "Truth" is eroded. Insecure and anxious, she begins to doubt that her voice and visions matter. Her role in society as a futurist and spiritual leader is jeopardized.

Apollo loses, too, though. Apollo, the god of prophecy, must go on without Cassandra's love or the use of her magnificent spiritual talents—especially important to him because of his deep connection to the Oracle of Pythia. By denying Cassandra, Apollo rejects an aspect of himself, cutting off, in effect, a part and product of his own divinity.

Myths are stories that detail patterns of human behavior repeated through millennia. Cassandra's myth reminds us that anti-war female voices do matter and must heard, even when caught in cultural cycles of "disbelief." Cassandra must not be silenced. According to myth, her protests must be voiced. If Cassandra's warnings had been heeded, there would have been no bloody Trojan War. The psychological impact on Cassandra to speak against the patriarchy was heavy. She was ostracized. But myth shows that Cassandra's female voice is needed to warn about war, to provide balance and insight, to shout of the dire ramifications of violent cycles: to try to save us.

Works Cited:

Aeschylus, *Agamemnon*. http://www.gutenberg.org/cache/epub/14417/pg14417.html. 11 July 2011.

Grimal, Pierre. *The Dictionary of Classical Mythology*. Trans. A.R. Maxwell-Hyslop. Oxford: Blackwell, 1996.

Hunter, James. "Cassandra."
http://www.pantheon.org/articles/c/cassandra.html. 11 July 2011.

Schapira, Laurie Layton. *The Cassandra Complex: Living with Disbelief.* Toronto, Inner City Books, 1988.

[28] For one view of Cassandra's death, see: http://www.uncg.edu/cla/myth/cassandra.htm.

6) HERA
The Hera Factor in Hillary's Run

(Note: "The Hera Factor in Hillary's Run" was originally published in The Los Angeles Times on July 11, 1999, pages M3 & M6. By seeing her candidacy through a mythic lens, I predicted Hillary Clinton's Senate campaign would resonate positively with voters. Her presidential campaign in 2007-2008 and her subsequent position as Secretary of State could be seen as part of the Hera archetype as outlined below. For a related essay, please see "America's Zeus.")

He was the most important man in the world. His daily decisions affected the entire cosmos. Officially, he was married, and their "sacred union" was constantly under public scrutiny. They presided together at stately functions, providing a handsome, regal example of what matrimony should be.

But he had extramarital affairs, lots of them. He couldn't seem to control himself when it came to women. He took great risks to arrange elicit sexual escapades, and that made his wife angry. She tried not to show it. She vowed to stay with him, to be "the good wife," even when it got embarrassing and humiliating. Young women complained; he was accused of rape. Gossip was repeated. Although their lives were filled with tension, she stayed with him.

Gradually, she began to assert her hand in public policy. She built a power base that rivaled her husband's realm.

A familiar synopsis? Yes, it is the story of the Greek goddess Hera. Many pundits have compared the Clinton White House during 1997-99 to a Greek tragedy, but few could name specifics that had the ring of truth. The Oval Office is our Mt. Olympus. Cast Monica S. Lewinsky as an Aphrodite-inspired mortal maiden and President Bill Clinton in the role of Zeus. That makes First Lady Hillary Rodham Clinton our modern-day Hera.

Hillary Clinton's likely Senate campaign echoes part of Hera's story, the final bid for individual power and integrity after years as a suffering "partner." Call it the Hera Factor. It explains why Hillary Clinton is raising money for a Senate campaign in the state of New York at a time when many wonder why she would want the annoyance of further public scrutiny.

For thousand of years, Hera has represented the archetype for "the good wife" in Western culture. Revered by women and the only married goddess on Mt. Olympus, she was the symbol of childbirth and marriage. Known for beauty, intelligence and a love of children, Hera embodied three phases of a woman's life: maiden, wife and matron, each with a separate identity. Originally Zeus' sister, their partnership took on a new dimension when they wed.

Zeus was the most powerful figure in the Greek pantheon, the symbol for justice and power. His weakness was his love life. He seduced goddesses, but the chief of the gods was just as happy to woo "mere mortals." Zeus took the magical form of a bull, swan or even a "shower of gold" to lure the mortal maidens he lusted after.

Hera never adjusted to Zeus' nonstop philandering. In "The Iliad," Hera joins a plot to keep Zeus in chains. The dynamic between Zeus and Hera shifts between anger, forgiveness and love. Hera's suffering seems to annoy Zeus further; she feels she has sacrificed her pride to stay with him, and he feels manipulated into guilt by her reaction. Some of the goddess' detractors label her quarrelsome, even vindictive, because of her dogged pursuit of her enemies and rivals, such as Io, whom Hera tortured with a horsefly until Io went mad. Gradually, Hera's image evolves to the steadfast spouse, the woman who suffers infidelity to ensure the longevity of her marriage.

But as she grows older, Hera's interests broaden into the realm of governing. She fights wars and becomes the protectress of the Argonauts, helping them pass between the Cyanean rocks. Devoted and passionate, Hera is a master player in the Olympian arena, able to govern without consulting other gods and capable of instigating action without her husband's approval. Hera has her own causes, her own purposes, her own cosmic game: She is her husband's equal.

Over the past year, we have watched Hillary Clinton stand by a president who cavorted with a mere mortal. The First Lady endured months of impeachment hearings, even allegations that her husband raped a woman. Throughout, she stumped for causes she believed in, weathering what must be the most public, sensationalized and documented marital-infidelity admission in modern history. So why would she want to run for the U.S. Senate now?

Because it's a win-win scenario for Hillary Clinton, from a psychological standpoint. Even if she loses the race, she will, merely by running for office, win her separateness from her husband as a viable political entity. If she is labeled a carpetbagger or is forced to talk about Whitewater again, she will do so as Hillary Clinton, candidate for Senate, no longer just the female component of the first couple. If she wins, all the better. She will become Sen. Clinton, the first former first lady to become a U.S. senator.

The Hera Factor helps explain a mythical context of Hillary Clinton's brave move; it may also help her candidacy resonate with New York voters on a deep, archetypal level, something that her probable contender, New York City Mayor Rudolph W. Giuliani, will have a tough time combating with mere rhetoric.

7) HESTIA
Martha Hearts Hestia

(*Note:* In December 18, 2000, I was interviewed by *The Los Angeles Times* in an article called "Together, My Magazine and I Can Redecorate Your Life" by Lynell George; the article was about women's magazines and branding. In the article, I commented: "When I think about Martha [Stewart], I think about Hestia, the goddess of Home." This essay was inspired by that conversation and published for the first time here.)

In Greek mythology, the archetype most associated with the home is Hestia, the virgin Goddess of the Hearth. Martha Stewart's brand may be seen as a commodification of Hestian ideals, updated for modern times; anything that concerns beautifying the home, preparing wonderful meals in the kitchen, and other facets of "domestic aesthetics" may be categorized as part of Hestia's domain.

HESTIA AND THE HEARTH

The name "Hestia" derives, according to Plato, from the Greek word *ousia*, which means "essence."[29] Hestia is essential, the spiritual "essence" of the home. It is also thought that "Hestia" derives from a root word that means "to burn."[30]

Known as the sister of Zeus and Hera, Hestia was granted special dispensation by Zeus never to leave Olympus for any reason; thus, it was thought that the spinster goddess Hestia was always "home."[31] Like the other Olympians, she was swallowed by her father Kronos as soon as she was born, and lived in his belly without her mother Rhea until her baby brother Zeus came to the rescue and launched the victorious war against the Titans. Hestia was the first to be swallowed—thus, the oldest—but the last to be rescued; see Hesiod's *Theogony* for more on this event.[32] Later, as we learn in "The Homeric Hymn to Aphrodite," the gods Poisedon and Apollo both tried to woo Hestia, but she rejected their marital offers, preferring life as a singleton.[33]

Hestia's genealogy is unclear, as if she *always* existed and *always* will. Considered the thirteenth Olympian, she was worshipped in ancient times.[34] Hestia was later incorporated into Olympus to symbolize the home as the "heart" of civilization. Hestia also was "post-Olympian" in that her archetype continued to rule the home after Zeus and company fell from favor. Rites related to Hestia are still practiced as part of a Greek New Year's ritual.[35]

Hestia was always a virgin, yet she came to symbolize a "mothering" figure who transcended biological function;[36] she was married to the home, and thus is truly a "house-wife." Frequently depicted in statues as hidden behind a long veil, Hestia's presence in a home is supposed to be concealed, invisible—so smooth that you can't see it. This relates to the "hidden" quality of the domestic arts which are so often assigned as gender-specific "feminine" duties, and which are often undervalued by contemporary society.

In ancient times, Hestia was thought to dutifully watch over one's house if proper daily rituals were performed; special rites were dedicated to Hestia related to the fire of the hearth, the "heart of the house." There are two Homeric Hymns addressed to Hestia. Hymn One begins:

> "Hestia, in the high dwellings of all,
> both deathless gods and men who walk the earth,
> you have gained an everlasting abode and highest honour:
> glorious is your portion and your right.
> For without you mortals hold no banquet,
> —where one does not duly pour sweet wine
> in offering to Hestia both first and last."[37]

The old expression "Keep the home fires burning" may be related to the power and function of the goddess Hestia, for as long as the physical and spiritual "heat" in one's home is well-tended, all is well within its walls for those who abide there. Hestia helped to keep homes "lit" in every way. Hestia was prayed to at the beginning and end of every meal, "no matter which divinity was being honored" at a feast.[38] Thus, Hestia represents the home as the beginning and the end, an "*alpha-omega*" distinctly domestic, soulful image. One starts the day at home with Hestia, and each night ends with her, too.

Hestia's archetype illustrates that the health of society-at-large depends on the tending of each home-hearth individually. There was an altar dedicated to Hestia "in the center of the council chambers of every Greek city, a communal hearth" of city hall.[39] Walter Burkert notes: "To have Hestia, Zeus, and Athena on the acropolis means having the hearth as the centre of the community, and the highest god and the representative of the city in proximity—an idealized Athens..."[40] These communal flames were sacred, generative, were passed on to new lands via lit torches: "it is from these fires that colonists carried the flame of the home city to new shores."[41]

Unlike many gods and goddesses residing in Mt. Olympus, Hestia is unassuming and calm; her only attachment is to the privacy of "home-work," away from the public sphere. There is one account that associates Hestia with Hermes, her brother (or nephew) who is thought to be the "kindler" of flames—the god of the road; Hestia protects the house, and Hermes protects all avenues that lead home.[42] First fruits, oil and wine were sacred to her.[43] Most of the stories about Hestia are lost or forgotten; or else, as some mythographers suggest, there were never any major stories about her at all, since she represents such a distinct concept in mythology—that of an archetype, in direct contrast to other figures in the Olympic pantheon, whose function is not related to active stories filled with adventure, battle, and romance, but instead to repose, repast, and quotidian contemplation. As Christine Downing writes in "Coming Home to Hestia": "Hestia is not present in the extraordinary as are other goddesses but in the midst of the ordinary and the mundane."[44]

Fire, which is part of Hestia's power, inspires meditation and reflection but also provides heat for cooking. In Greek, the word *estia* is a hearth, a household, a family or a gathering place.[45] The hearth was considered essential for a house as, before ovens and stoves, food was cooked on or near the hearth. It was also the central source of heat for a home. Therefore, heat is seen as "essential," and directly related to the concept of sustenance, nurturance, food, survival. But there is also a "phoenix rising from the ashes" alchemical association with fire, as it may spark new beginnings, even if it burns in a destructive way, paving the way for new creation. So Hestia's fire provides a place for physical and spiritual renewal in the home.

Gaston Bachelard, in *The Psychoanalysis of Fire* (1938), describes learning how to properly light a hearth by observing his father's ritualized approach: "He would take great care in arranging the logs over the kindling chips, and in slipping the handful of shavings between the andirons..."[46] Bachelard saw it as a personal *rite de passage* when he, as a young adult, finally took on this duty himself—that of lighting his own personal hearth: "...I was eighteen years old. It was only when I lived alone that I became master of my own hearth. But I still take special pride in *the art of kindling* I learned from my father. I think I would rather fail to teach a good philosophy lesson than to fail to light my morning fire."[47]

There are two central rituals which show how important Hestia was to a girl's future in ancient times. The first ritual is related to weddings. As Stephanie A. Demetrakopolous describes in her essay "Hestia, Goddess of the Hearth: Notes on an Oppressed Archetype," a "bride's mother lit a torch at her own household altar" and waved it before a young couple entered their new domicile, then lit the first flame in the new hearth.[48] This rite symbolized the transference of mother-to-daughter's hearth-to-hearth, heart-to-heart. It was also a rite of passage for the daughter, a signal that she had come of age: she'd acquired her own hearth. This ritual reinforces the hearth as related to fulfilling a new wife's dreams, and entering a new, more mature phase of life.

The second ritual is called the *Amphidromia*, and is related to birth. When a newborn infant was five days old, he or she was carried around the hearth as a symbol of the child's admission into the ways of the family. Some accounts say the father ran around the hearth with the child; other versions point to gifts and feasting as part of the ceremony.[49] In some way, our modern custom of "baby showers" is most likely related to this ancient rite. Thus, Hestia's influence was needed to bind the family at the hearth, where the fire of the heart must be tended. For a woman, this meant that all hopes were high for a healthy newborn, blessed by Hestia's hearth. Thus, there is a symbolic reproduction association here for women and the hearth.

Hestia was also known to the Romans as "Vesta"; in her Roman incarnation, she was the basis for the famous "Vestal Virgins," who were seen as holy and pure—female sacrificial figures.

MARTHA STEWART LIVING

Martha Stewart's brand intersects the primary aspects of Hestia, promising us a beauty in the home, showing us ways to give the home a special flare, and a place to cook wonderful meals for friends and family, and how to decorate to make rituals special. If you pick up a copy of *Martha Stewart Living*, or visit marthastewart.com, many of the articles are enticing recipes, or "entertaining tips." Martha Stewart's brand is multi-platformed, a combination of television, bestselling books, several magazines, and a website.

The logo at the top of Martha Stewart's website, marthastewart.com, is a green circle, enclosed with a white inner circle. Martha Stewart's name is around the interior circumference.[50] Hestia, too, is linked to the image of the circle. Demetrakopoulos writes: "The major symbol that recurs with Hestia is the circle, such as we saw above in the circular fire of the Vedics."[51]

Another feature of Stewart's website is the "Daily Inspiration" column, which highlights seasonal recipes, herb usage, and tips about the "family room." Other buttons lead to advice about "weddings," "home-keeping," and "baby shower themes." Headlines include "House Proud," "Holidays," and "Whole Living."[52] "Whole Living," another Martha Stewart magazine, is a green, organic lifestyle approach, "body+soul in balance."[53] Adding the aspect of "soul" to the Martha Stewart mix links her brand to the archetype of Hestia at a deeper level.

In a typical "Table of Contents" page from a *Martha Stewart Living* magazine, such as the August 2011 "Dig Into Summer" issue, cooking, entertaining, and home decoration are the foci of most articles. "Mad Hungry, Talking Turkey" considers many ways to prepare roast turkey. "Home Design, Present Perfect with Kevin Sharkey" details how to prepare your home for weekend summer guests. "What's For Dinner?" is a regular feature of every *MSL* issue.[54] Stewart has also promoted the value of the hearth to contemporary living. As she commented to Kevin Sharkey in a January 2011 issue of *Martha Stewart Living*: "Fireplaces are a gorgeous and a traditional location in a home that is a perfect place to gather around when you are with friends and family. Not everyone living in New York City is lucky enough to have a fireplace in their home—and many who have one don't take advantage of using it. Decorations around a fireplace can make the room more cozy and elegant—decorating your mantels can be done every season and it can add color and life to your room."[55] This may be seen as related to a ritualization of the hearth; it is also an acknowledgement that we have, in modern life, lost the concept of the centrifugal hearth.

Martha describes herself as a "businessperson in addition to a creator of domestic arts."[56] Her brand and business promote the values of home that are similar to those found in the ancient archetype of the goddess Hestia; Hestian energy, per Martha Stewart, is seen as key to the "inner fire" of a home, and also to its grace. In the Homeric "Hymn 24 to Hestia," there is an appeal for Hestia's blessing: "Hestia, you who tend the holy house of the lord Apollo, the Far-shooter at goodly Pytho, with soft oil dripping ever from your locks, come now into this house, come, having one mind with Zeus the all-wise—draw near, and withal bestow grace upon my song."[57]

Works Cited

Bachelard, Gaston. *The Psychoanalysis of Fire*. Trans. Alan C.M. Ross. Boston: Beacon Press, 1964.

Burkert, Walter. *Greek Religion*. Trans. John Raffan. Cambridge, MA, Harvard UP, p. 128.

Demetrakopoulos, Stephanie. "Hestia, Goddess of the Hearth: Notes on an Oppressed Archetype." *Spring Journal*, 1979. 55-75.

Downing, Christine. "Coming Home to Hestia." *Journey Through Menopause: A Personal Rite of Passage*. New York: Crossroad, 1987. 131-164.

Evelyn-White, Hugh G. Translator (Public Domain). "To Hestia—Homeric Hymn to Hestia." http://ancienthistory.about.com/library/bl/bl_text_homerhymn_hestia2.htm 20 August 2011.

"Hestia." *Funk and Wagnalls Standard Dictionary of Folklore, Mythology, and Legend*. Ed. Maria Leach. San Francisco: Harper SanFrancisco, 1984. 495.

Grimal, Pierre. *The Dictionary of Classical Mythology*. Trans. A.R. Maxwell-Hyslop. Oxford, U.K.: Blackwell Publishers, 1996.

Sharkey, Kevin. "Snow in New York City, and Fireplaces To Warm Up Next To." 13 Jan. 2011. http://homedesign.marthastewart.com/2011/01/snow-in-new-york-city-and-fireplaces-to-warm-up-next-to.html. 20 August 2011.

Stewart, Martha. Interview with Larry King Live, CNN transcript. July 19, 2004. http://transcripts.cnn.com/TRANSCRIPTS/0407/19/lkl.00.html.

[29] Downing, p. 134.
[30] Demetrakopoulos, p. 61.
[31] Grimal, p. 123.
[32] Demetrakopoulos, p. 56.
[33] Demetrakopolous, p. 63.
[34] Downing, p. 140.
[35] Demetrakopoulos, p. 56.
[36] Downing, pps. 146-147.
[37] Evelyn-White.
[38] Downing , p. 138/Demetrakopolous, p. 62.
[39] Downing, p. 148.
[40] Burkert, p. 335.
[41] "Hestia."
[42] Demetrakopolous, p. 59.
[43] "Hestia."
[44] Downing, p. 134.
[45] Demetrakopolous, p. 61.
[46] Bachelard, p. 8.
[47] Bachelard, p. 9.
[48] Demetrakopolous, pps. 61-62.
[49] Demetraokopolous, p. 62.
[50] As viewed on August 20, 2011.
[51] Demetraopolous, p. 71.
[52] www.marthastewart.com, accessed on August 20, 2011.
[53] www.wholeliving.com, accessed on August 20, 2011.
[54] *Martha Stewart Living*, August 2011.
[55] "Snow in New York City And Fireplaces to Warm Up Next To." January 13, 2011. http://homedesign.marthastewart.com/2011/01/snow-in-new-york-city-and-fireplaces-to-warm-up-next-to.html. Accessed on August 20, 2011.
[56] "Interview with Martha Stewart," Larry King Live. CNN. July 19, 2004. http://transcripts.cnn.com/TRANSCRIPTS/0407/19/lkl.00.html. Accessed on Aug. 20, 2011.
[57] Evelyn-White, Hugh G. (trans.) "Hymn 24 to Hestia." Perseus Hopper. Tufts University. Accessed on April 6, 2012. http://www.perseus.tufts.edu/hopper/text?doc=Perseus%3atext%3a1999.01.0138%3ahymn%3d24.

8) HYGIEIA AND ASCLEPIUS
The Holiness of Health

(Note: This essay was first published in Mythopoetry Scholar, Volume One, on January 1, 2010, Mythopoetry.com.)

In the eighteenth century, Ben Franklin wrote in his *Poor Richard's Almanack*: "Early to bed, early to rise makes a man healthy, wealthy and wise." Centuries later, much of our civic conversations in America about "health" center on issues related to its cost and its commodification; the "wealth" or "financial" aspects of health, one might say, dominate the twenty-first century U.S. political dialogue. This limited approach excludes the spiritual wisdom and psychic import of health; in order to understand its meaning from an archetypal perspective, it is important to unpack the divine aspects of its origins.

In mythology, there are many examples of "the sacred" connected to "healing," as related to medicine, health and the gods and goddesses.

The etymology in English of the word "health" is rooted in Old English and Old Norse words: the Old English "hale" or whole; the Old Norse "heill" for healthy; the Old English "halig" and the Old Norse "helge" for holy, sacred, dedicated to the gods; and the Old English "haelen" which means to heal.[58] In English, "health" is tied to the gods linguistically. *The Oxford English Dictionary* lists a use of the noun "health," circa 1000 C.E., as denoting a "spiritual, moral or mental soundness of being; salvation."[59] "Salvation" signals that health is a transformative force that can protect and save; it suggests a religious, spiritual context and lexicon.

The link between ancient myth, healing, and deities is evident in many traditions. In ancient Egypt, for example, Imhotep, a key physician and vizier to Pharoah Zozer (circa 2600 B.C.E.), was worshipped as a god by later dynasties—one of few mortals to be elevated to divine status, based on his ability to heal. Michael T. Kennedy writes in *A Brief History of Disease, Science & Medicine*: "By the sixth century he [Imhotep] had replaced Thoth as the god of healing."[60] Sir William Osler, the "Father of Modern Medicine," identifies Imhotep as the Father of Medicine, "the first figure of a physician to stand out clearly from the mists of antiquity."[61] The "Father of Medicine" was a god.

In Greek myth, healing is a central component in the worship of Apollo. He was given the title of *"Epikourios"* ["helper/healer"], and was also called *"Iatros"* ["doctor"]. Walter Burkert, in *Greek Religion*, observes: "The god of the healing hymn might well be a magician god; Apollo is just the opposite, a god of purifications and cryptic oracles...the god of purifications must also be an oracle god—however much the function of oracles later extends beyond the domain of cultic prescriptions."[62] From an archetypal angle, Apollo's cultic prescriptions are divine, and intended to purify or "solve" a situation or problem. Consider: may comparisons be drawn between ancient oracular advice and modern medicinal prescriptions from doctors for healing herbs, lifestyle change recommendations and pharmaceuticals?

It is Asclepius, the son of Apollo, who is most remembered today as the "medicine" god of the Greek pantheon. Worldwide, many medical organizations still use a single entwined snake logo, related to Asclepius' rod, as a branding symbol; these groups include the American Medical Association, the Australian Medical Association, the British Royal Army Medical Corps, the Canadian Medical Association, the World Health Organization, the Pakistan Army Medical Corps, the United States Air Force Medical Corps, among others.[63] The twinned winged snakes on the Caduceus of Hermes were, for many years, mistakenly conflated with the Rod of Asclepius, highlighting a "healer" aspect of Hermes' messenger-trickster archetype, and lending a "trickster" component to medical branding and advertising.[64] Thus, two gods, both Asclepius and Hermes, are associated with this modern symbol of medicine and healing.

There are several versions of the birth myth of Apollo's healer-son Asclepius. Pindar's version seems to be the most familiar; young Asclepius was miraculously birthed on a burning pyre from the womb of his mother, the dead princess Coronis, whom Apollo punished for her infidelity to the god. His mother, in this version, was royal. In another version, which is thought to explain the location of Asclepius' extensive sanctuary at Epidaurus, Asclepius is the abandoned grandchild of the nomadic thief Phlegyas, whose chief purpose in life is to steal wealth. Phlegyas' daughter had a secret mountain *rendezvous* with Apollo. Asclepius' mother, in this rendition, was tied to thievery. In either case, Asclepius was born at Epidaurus, and left to his own devices. A shepherd found him, but could see immediately that the child was divine; Asclepius was encircled by brilliant light. The shepherd left the god-child alone, to survive on his own with the help of a she-goat and a dog. Later, Asclepius was taught about medicine by the centaur Chiron, and his greatest medical feat was his unique ability to revive the dead.[65] It was his ability to resurrect others that angered Zeus, who feared Asclepius' powers. Zeus killed Asclepius with a thunderbolt; vengefully, Apollo retaliated by killing the Cyclopes.

Asclepius' reach extended beyond Greece; the healing powers of Asclepius were so legendary that he, as a deity, was introduced in Rome to avert a plague in 293 B.C.E.[66]

At Epidaurus, a school of medicine flourished in Asclepius' name; Hippocrates was among those who studied there.[67] The time-honored Hippocratic Oath in its original text began with a nod to two gods and two goddesses who share a common lineage: "I swear by Apollo, the healer, Asclepius, Hygieia, and Panacea, and I take to witness all the gods, all the goddesses, to keep according to my ability and my judgment, the following Oath and agreement…"[68] The Hippocratic Oath, in a modern form, is still considered relevant to the field of medical ethics. In the ancient version of the oath, the physician first acknowledges key deities before addressing the physician's duties. There was no medical licensing in antiquity; the oath functioned as a code of honor.[69] Who to witness a sacred vow for healers but the gods and goddesses?

Just as gods and goddesses were associated with healing, so they were associated with the opposite: illness. Burkert writes: "The most oppressive crisis for the individual is illness. Many different gods or heroes are capable of sending illness in their wrath…Apollo's son Asklepios proved his competence, particularly in dealing with the troubles of the individual, and thus overshadowed other healing gods and heroes."[70]

The path to healing for an individual, via Asclepian rituals at Epidaurus in ancient Greece, usually involved a three day stay at the site. On the first day, the patient had to seek purity, abstain from sexual relations, and reject specific foods. Next, preliminary offerings were made; wearing a laurel wreath,[71] the patient made an animal sacrifice to Apollo, and a pig sacrifice to Asclepius, along with money donated on the Asclepian altar. Before the evening "incubation," three cakes were readied. Two were for Tyche and Mnemosyne [Success and Recollection] and one for Themis [Right

Order]. If cured, the patient left behind the laurel wreath, and thanked the gods. Burkert writes: "...a successful outcome was readily accepted as the good gift of the gods that confirm the value of piety."[72] This Asclepian ritual could be seen as similar to some contemporary medical procedures: preparation for a surgery or procedure may involve the elimination of certain foods and activities beforehand; some payment is required in advance; in the end, we hope for success, a sound mind, and the completion of the correct procedures.

The goddess Hygieia [Health] was the daughter of Asclepius, and was usually depicted in his entourage.[73] Hygieia was often shown, in artwork, holding a snake in her hands. As part of the ritual of Asclepius at Epidaurus, it was possible to drink directly of the goddess Hygieia—in her healing liquid form, consisting of a wheat, honey and oil concoction.[74] Perhaps the modern practice of "drinking to one's health" could be seen as related to this ancient ritual.

The goddess Panacea [Cure-All] was another daughter of Asclepius, sister to Hygieia: "she symbolizes the universal power of healing through herbs."[75] Over 300 temples and sanitoriums were built to honor Asclepius, his goddess-daughters, and his wife Epione, the goddess who could relieve pain.[76] The word "Panacea" is still in use by physicians today.

For the sake of our collective well-being, our understanding of "health" in the twenty-first century must be "remembered" to aspects of its mythic origins. The "Father of Medicine" is an Egyptian doctor-god Imhotep. The western concept of health is impacted significantly by Greek archetypes related to healing and medicine; the influences of Apollo, Asclepius, Hermes, Hygieia and Panacea are still evident today. Medical logos, ethics, and some practices/traditions are related to these deities. In English, the linguistic roots of the word "health" remind us of its divine essence.

It is possible to "re-vision" health in the twenty-first century. But in order to do so, it is imperative that we honor its sacred status in the human psyche, in equal measure to modern practical concerns.

---

[58] "health." *Online Etymology Dictionary*. Douglas Harper, Historian. 30 Nov. 2009. <Dictionary.com http://dictionary.reference.com/browse/health>.
[59] "health." *Oxford English Dictionary*, 2nd Ed., 1989. 30 Nov. 2009. http://dictionary.oed.com/cgi/entry/50103662?query_type=word&queryword=HEALTH&first=1&max_to_show=10&sort_type=alpha&result_place=2&search_id=Uthu-beNzw9-9196&hilite=50103662.
[60] Kennedy, Michael T. *A Brief History of Disease, Science and Medicine*. Mission Viejo CA: Asklepiad Press, 2004, p. 15.
[61] "Imhotep." Wikipedia. 22 Dec. 2009. http://en.wikipedia.org/wiki/Imhotep.
[62] Burkert, Walter. *Greek Religion*. Cambridge, MA: Harvard UP, 1985, p. 147.
[63] "Rod of Asclepius." Wikipedia.org. 22 Dec. 2009. http://en.wikipedia.org/wiki/Rod_of_Asclepius.
[64] For an example of the Caduceus of Hermes, please see: http://en.wikipedia.org/wiki/File:Caduceus.svg.
[65] Grimal, Pierre. *The Dictionary of Classical Mythology*. Trans. A. R. Maxwell-Hyslop. Oxford: Blackwell, 1996, pps. 62-63.
[66] Hughes, J. Donald. *Pan's Travail: Environmental Problems of the Ancient Greeks and Romans*. Baltimore: Johns Hopkins UP, 1994, p. 186.
[67] Grimal, Pierre. *The Dictionary of Classical Mythology*. Trans. A. R. Maxwell-Hyslop. Oxford: Blackwell, 1996, p. 63.
[68] "Hippocratic Oath." Wikipedia.org. 22 Dec. 2009. http://en.wikipedia.org/wiki/Hippocratic_Oath.
[69] Pomeroy, Sarah, et al. *Ancient Greece: A Political, Social, and Cultural History*. New York: Oxford University Press, 1999, p. 462.
[70] Burkert, Walter. *Greek Religion*. Cambridge, MA: Harvard UP, 1985, p. 267.
[71] The laurel wreath was sacred to Apollo.
[72] Burkert, Walter. *Greek Religion*. Cambridge, MA: Harvard UP, 1985, pps. 267-268.
[73] Grimal, Pierre. *The Dictionary of Classical Mythology*. Trans. A. R. Maxwell-Hyslop. Oxford: Blackwell, 1996, p. 219.
[74] Burkert, Walter. *Greek Religion*. Cambridge, MA: Harvard UP, 1985, p. 268.

[75] Grimal, Pierre. *The Dictionary of Classical Mythology.* Trans. A. R. Maxwell-Hyslop. Oxford: Blackwell, 1996, p. 141.
[76] Brooke, Elizabeth. *Women Healers: Portraits of Herbalists, Physicians and Midwives.* Rochester, VT; Healing Arts Press, 1995, pps. 10-11.

9) THE MUSES
Muse-Worthy:
Francine Prose's *The Lives of the Muses*

(Note: This essay was originally published in "The Muses," Spring Journal 70, March 2004, pps. 15-23.)

In her 2002 bestseller *The Lives of the Muses: Nine Women and the Artists They Inspired*, author Francine Prose examines the sociocultural evolution of the Muse archetype during the past two hundred and fifty years. Prose selects nine women who lived from the late eighteenth century through the twentieth century, and who had direct connections to prominent male artists (two painters, two photographers, three writers, a choreographer, and a musician). She offers a single chapter on each of her nine female "muses"; each section, in effect, serves as a separate case study.

Prose raises many provocative questions about the state of modern "musedom," including: what is the definition of a "muse" in contemporary culture? What is the effect of twentieth century feminism on our understanding of a female muse's role in the male artist's creative process? What are key issues of gender-sexual prejudices, and patriarchal attitudes related to being a muse, e.g., can a man be a muse, and can a woman be a muse to another woman? What exactly are the quotidian functions of a muse? What is the penultimate effect of the male gaze on the female muse in artist-model/writer-subject paradigms? When is gratitude for and acknowledgement of a muse's contribution to the artist's *oeuvre* expressed (or not)? What are the boundaries of a muse's social status, which often shift from the exciting, even romantic categories of "secret inspirer" or "unofficial collaborator," to the less rewarding slot of "art wife"? Does motherhood interfere with or even preclude "musedom?" What propels the competitive struggle between artist and muse, especially when the muse decides to become an artist in her own right? And finally, what brings about the inevitable end of a muse's influence in the life or career of the artist? For, as Prose points out in the final third of her book: "Except in extremely rare cases—Gala Dalí's, for example—tenure is not an option in the career of the muses."[77]

In her nine-woman study, Prose profiles Hester Thrale's connection to author/dictionary creator Dr. Samuel Johnson; the child muse Alice Liddell's effect on *Wonderland* creator "Lewis Carroll," a.k.a. Charles Dodgson; Elizabeth Siddal's tie to artist Gabriel Dante Rossetti and the Pre-Raphaelites; Lou Andreas-Salomé's serial "muse" associations with philosopher Frederick Nietzsche, poet Rainer Maria Rilke, and psychology's Sigmund Freud; Gala Dalí's powerful link to artist-husband Salvador Dalí; Lee Miller's three-year affair with photographer Man Ray; Charis Weston Wilson's influence over photographer-husband Edmund Weston; Suzanne Farrell's complex artistic and personal relationship with ballet choreographer-dancer George Ballanchine; and Yoko Ono's highly publicized muse-to-partner love affair with former Beatle John Lennon.

Although Prose's introduction to the book includes mythological genealogies and perspectives, she makes no attempt to correlate the traditional domains of the nine muses (Tragedy,

Comedy/Dance, Mime, History, Astronomy, etc.) directly to her chosen subjects.

Definition of a Muse

Why do we, as humans, need muses at all? Prose posits: "The logical solution to the mystery of creation is divine intervention—a simple enough explanation, except for the dizzying speed with which our ideas about divinity changes from era to era, from culture to culture. The Greeks assumed that a deity had to be involved."[78]

Prose explores the mysterious etymology of "muse," tracing its possible roots to ancient terms for "ardor," "mind," "memory," or "mountain."[79] She does not address the trinitarianism of the muses in her myth genealogy. Yet their magical "threeness" is central to the archetype; in some early accounts, there were only three muses, "analogous to the Graces," and this triadic base is present in the current "three times three" construction which was standardized in the classical period.[80] Nor does Prose detail the classical muses' collective function as "divine singers," or their service to Apollo, in some accounts, and Orpheus and the cult of Dionysus, in others.[81] Instead, she focuses on the more generalized inspirational activities of "nurturing, sustaining, supporting, encouraging" as key aspects of the muse archetype.[82] She argues for "inspiration as a social and communal activity."[83] The etymology of "inspire" seems relevant here as well; it derives from Old French *enspirer* and the Latin *inspirare,* which means "to breathe or blow upon or into."[84] The divine, singing muse is capable of breathing life directly into our souls.

Prose constructs a continuum of human muses; her trajectory extends from the Greek immortals to medieval mortals. She references Petrarch's Laura numerous times in the introduction and throughout the book; Dante's Beatrice is another recurring medieval example that Prose connects to her modern nine, and most especially to the union of Dante Rossetti and Elizabeth Siddal.

Early on, Prose cautions that "romantic fantasy," as part of the teeming thrall of musedom which enjoins muse-to-artist and artist-to-muse, activates the creative psyche more than actual "erotic gratification."[85] Prose identifies the durability of "the power of longing" versus "the thrill of possession" in these special relationships.[86] She also highlights the importance of Eros and love in the life of the muse.

Real Women As Muses

Prose begins her study with a chapter on Hester Thrale and Dr. Samuel Johnson, a tale set near central London. Due to health issues, severe melancholia, and the hospitable goodwill of the upwardly mobile Thrales, Dr. Johnson began a sixteen-year stay as a house guest in the Thrales' home in 1766. She and her husband Henry took great pity on the widowed, sickly Johnson; Hester helped to nurse the semi-invalid through illnesses and to transcribe his books. There were rumors of a love affair between Hester and the doctor, although when Henry died, Johnson and Thrale did not marry. Thrale published her own account of life with the dictionary creator in 1785 (*Anecdotes of the Late Samuel Johnson*), but Prose identifies a "code of silence" credo in Thrale's story, to which many muse-women adhere: that of protecting the artist and his reputation, especially after his death.

There were some things which Thrale never divulged about Johnson, including an explanation of a curious relic leftover from their years of co-habitation—a padlock owned by the doctor, and entrusted to her care in 1768—which Prose intimates was either used in masochistic rituals, or perhaps was a simply metaphor for the spiritual-sexual bondage which exists between muse-artist.

In another part of England, Alice Liddell's reign as a child muse to Charles Dodgson, whose pen name was "Lewis Carroll," began when she was about seven; he was twenty-seven or twenty-eight. Dodgson photographed her in a provocative pose and costume for his "Portrait of Alice Liddell as the Beggar Child" (circa 1858 or early 1859), a picture which Alfred, Lord Tennyson praised as the most beautiful photograph he'd ever seen.

Alice's father was a Dean of Christ Church College in Oxford, where Dodgson was employed teaching mathematics. Dodgson often ingratiated himself with families, using his photography skills as a way to get acquainted with them; and so it was with the Liddell household. Dodgson invented the *Alice in Wonderland* and *Alice Through the Looking Glass* tales to amuse Alice when she was ten, during a "golden afternoon" spent rowing on the river with Dodgson and her sisters Lorina and Edith. Later, Dodgson wrote and illustrated the Alice stories to win her affections; he presented them to her as gifts, even after her mother had forbidden Dodgson to see Alice again, for reasons that have never been fully disclosed. A missing page, torn from Dodgson's diary, is thought to detail his perspective on the mysterious incident; Alice herself adhered to a lifetime of the muse's "code of silence" and never revealed exactly what passed between them, although there has long been speculation about a spurned marriage proposal or an attempted romantic involvement that the Liddell family deemed inappropriate.

Was Alice Liddell's musedom wholly an "unconscious" one, due to her youth, her muse role charged by the possibly pedophiliac nature of Dodgson's fixation on her? Prose asks: "How much does the beggar child know? Where do we draw the line between the sacred and the carnal? And whose idea, whose decision was it to slide Alice's dress off her shoulders?"[87] The effects of the male gaze and objectification of the muse is especially relevant here, and in the next British muse story as well.

Elizabeth Siddal Rossetti (née Siddall) was a lower class woman of twenty-one years who lived in London, and worked as a milliner's assistant in a Cranbourne Alley shop when she was discovered in 1850 by Pre-Raphaelite painter Walter Deverell. "Lizzie" became a model for the Pre-Raphaelite Brotherhood, posing first for Deverell's "Twelfth Night." Prose speculates that Dante Gabriel Rossetti had a "Dante" complex, and that Siddal's passionate relationship with him was partially a result of his Dante-Beatrice obsession: Lizzie became his artistic and personal fixation. He featured her in his paintings, and pursued her romantically, undaunted by differences in "class." Perhaps his fervor was also fanned by Lizzie's talents; she, too, painted and wrote poetry. Not content merely to "model," Siddal created art alongside the legendary P.R.B—transforming from muse-to-artist in her own right: a tricky *rite de passage* through which other Prose "muses" venture in the twentieth century.

Siddal died tragically, in 1862, of an overdose of the opiate laudanum; Rossetti impulsively threw a book of poems into her casket at her burial. Seven years later, he had her body exhumed so that he could retrieve the poetry. Prose alludes to this as an artistic necrophilial connection between Rossetti and his dead muse-wife; the ability of his muse to inspire Rossetti, many years after her passing, evokes further comparisons to Dante/Beatrice and Rossetti/Siddal.

Russian writer Lou Andreas-Salomé could be seen as the quintessential "serial" muse, as she, for many decades, affected the lives of Nietzsche, philosopher Paul Rée, Rilke, and Freud—even as she was eventually married to professor Friedrich Carl Andreas. Andreas-Salomé was a professional writer, and later an analyst. Andreas-Salomé valued her career; she felt it was equally as important as those of her stellar cadre. According to Prose, Lou always fought "for self-determination."[88] Born in 1861, and ever the "free spirit," Andreas-Salomé died in 1937, two years before Freud did. Their friendship was strong in the last years of their lives; they discussed the "sunny aspects" of aging, menopause, and how the late-life departure of Eros signified a final stage reminiscent of childhood.

In the portraits of Gala Dalí and Charis Weston, Prose offers two different looks at the transition from "muse" to "art-wife." After Gala Eluard's first date with Salvador Dalí (while she was still married to Paul Eluard), she exclaimed to her future husband: "My little boy! We shall never leave each other!"[89] Charis Weston, who began as a model for her husband Edward, first saw the photographer from across a crowded room at a party; they exchanged discreet glances and he made his way to her, asking to be introduced.

Prose says that Gala Dalí enacted the role of "Surrealist sex goddess" to achieve her wife-musedom; Charis Weston Wilson became a "muse-memoirist" later in life, forty years after her former husband's death, thus breaking the "code of silence" by writing a tell-all book (with Wendy Madar) entitled *Through Another Lens*, which was published in 1998.

Prose identifies Lee Miller's three-year affair with photographer Man Ray, which began when Miller modeled for him, as a seminal tutelage which sparked Miller's own career as a World War II correspondent and ground-breaking female photojournalist. Miller emblematizes, for Prose, the modern muse-woman, who "could outgrow her sacred obligation to further the work of the artist and go on to lead a more independent life. She could even, potentially, *become* an artist in her own right."[90]

In the final chapters, Prose probes the state of the muse at the end of the twentieth century through two stories: prima ballerina's Suzanne Farrell's relationship to Balanchine, and artist-musician Yoko One's marriage to Lennon. In both cases, the artistic talents of the "women-muses" were in evidence before their inspirational tenures began, though they gained greater recognition through these artistic-personal partnerships.

Prose quotes ballet star Jacques D'Amboise, who, in recalling the magic of Farrell onstage in the 1960's, says she danced "'like a demon—but a goddess.'"[91] Such a description brings to mind the mythological "daimon" and its role in sparking genius; some of the storminess of Lennon and Ono's competitive union could attributed to dueling daimons. One wonders: What is the connection, if any, between the artist's daimon and his/her muse? Ono's story, the last one in the book, epitomizes the path of the powerful feminist-muse, and puts as a final, post-modern (albeit tragic) spin on the archetype.

The Enduring Value of the Muse

In her short Afterword, Prose concludes that love is the most enduring aspect of musedom—that these nine women loved and were loved, and that passion and love are foundational to creativity. Perhaps so.

But Prose achieves something even more important than this final observation about love and creativity in *The Lives of the Muses*: she builds an effective, highly entertaining case for the viability and mutability of the muse archetype in the modern world. She proves that the muse has value still in our lives, and in the artistic process. Prose argues for muse-worthiness, demanding acknowledgement of the muse's spiritual, artistic, and cultural currency in the twenty-first century. After reading *The Lives of the Muses*, one feels a sort of archetypal wonderment: for a myth retold, regenerated, and reclaimed.

[77] Francine Prose. *The Lives of the Muses: Nine Women and the Artists They Inspired.* (New York: HarperCollins, 2002), 271.
[78] Prose, 3.
[79] Prose, 3.
[80] Pierre Grimal (trans. A. R. Maxwell-Hyslop). *The Dictionary of Classical Mythology* (London: Blackwell, 1996), p. 298.
[81] Grimal, p. 297.
[82] Prose, p. 12.
[83] Prose, p. 21.
[84] *Oxford English Dictionary* Online, "Inspire." 5 Jan. 2004. <http:dictionary.oed.com/cgi/entry/00118192?single=1&query_type+word&queryword=i nspire&edition=2e&first=1&max_to_show=10>.
[85] Prose, p. 18.
[86] Prose, p. 17.
[87] Prose, p. 73.
[88] Prose, p. 168.
[89] Prose, p. 195.
[90] Prose, p. 230.
[91] Prose, p. 303.

10) ZEUS
America's Zeus

(Note: I have long been fascinated with the historical American association of Zeus to the Presidency. In 1840, sculptor Horatio Greenough depicted George Washington on a giant Throne of Zeus, modeled after "Zeus Olympios" in ancient Greece; this statue of George Washington ["Enthroned Washington"] is now in the Smithsonian. In Hodgenville, Kentucky, a neo-Greek temple Memorial Building was opened in 1911 to mark the birthplace of Abraham Lincoln ["Abraham Lincoln Birthplace National Historical Park"]. At the Lincoln Memorial on the National Mall in Washington, D.C., Lincoln is housed in the "Temple of Zeus" near the Reflecting Pool; this image is on the back of the five dollar bill. The neo-classical columns on the White House remind us of Zeus' associations to every elected occupant, and why the archetype is always relevant to the American presidency—including the concept of "power leaks," a shadow side of Zeus. This essay was originally published in Newsday on January 14, 2001, with the title "The Clinton Years: America's Zeus," page B5. For a related essay, please see "The Hera Factor in Hillary's Run.")

Mythology provides us with patterns of human behavior as depicted in ancient stories and images. We read these stories, and we see these images. They are registered in our collective psyche and so ingrained that when there are parallels in modern times these tales resonate more forcefully. They guide our psychology—our personal choices.

For Bill Clinton, the archetype most present is Zeus. As the most powerful figure in the Greek pantheon, Zeus had the ability to transform and shapeshift, and he often did so in pursuit of his goals. Married to Hera, Zeus occasionally had a few crazy affairs—one hundred and fifteen according to some mythologists.[92] To pursue many of these women, mostly mortal women, Zeus morphed into a shower of gold, a swan and a bull. And when fighting the giant monster Typhon in the war with the Titans, all of Zeus' tendons were cut out of his body and given to a female dragon. Things looked bleak. Then Hermes and Pan stole the tendons back. Zeus was able to restore his own muscles and fly instantly into the sky with a horse-drawn chariot in order to continue the battle with Typhon. Zeus eventually won the battle. In doing that, he united a disparate group of siblings in order to overthrow the Titans.

Benevolent and responsible, Zeus was good at building alliances. Clinton transformed throughout his two terms in order to pursue his political goals. He shapeshifted from the left to the center. After initial defeats, he regained strength and fought on. Recovering from early setbacks in health-care and gays-in-the-military policies, Clinton helmed the longest economic expansion in the nation's history. He presided over significant strides in the federal budget debt and created 22 million new jobs. Clinton forged bipartisan alliances—his 1997 Budget Act is a case in point. And what of the impeachment hearings and Monica Lewinsky? Merely another facet of the Zeus-power leader archetype, and the American people knew it. Zeus' power and authority, as King of the Cosmos, were never put into question as a result of the flings. The flings were expected. Although the GOP tried hard to make Americans question Clinton's abilities, his job approval ratings and popularity remained high throughout his two terms.

The final aspect of Clinton's legacy is Sen. Hillary Clinton. If Clinton was our Zeus, then Hillary as been our Hera.

Hera was initially the model of the good wife in the Greek pantheon. She suffered greatly because of her husband's indiscretions. Eventually, she made a final bid for individual power and integrity. She became her husband's equal, involved in furthering her own causes. Hera became the protectress of Jason and the Argonauts and was involved in the Trojan War.

Hillary Clinton, after withstanding the public humiliation of her husband's infidelity, has become her own woman with a separate political identity—a symbol of women's rights. Recent polls show she is the most admired woman in the country. Bill Clinton will leave office with an unprecedented first: Six more years of Clintonian influence in politics after the end of his administration due to his spouse's success in the election.

For eight years, Clinton felt our pain and we felt his power. Clinton's archetypal ties to Zeus ensure that he will always be remembered by the collective American psyche as a dynamic, strong, yet complex leader. The lasting impression—already familiar to us from ancient patterns—will resonate in a deeper way.

---

[92] Cited in Walter Burkert's *Greek Religion*. Trans. John Raffan. Cambridge, MA, Harvard UP, p. 128.

PART TWO: MYTH MISCELLANY

11) The Gaming of Love

(Note: Relationship game shows have been on the television for a long time. But shows dating from the 1960's, like "The Dating Game" and "The Newlywed Game," are mild in comparison to romance reality programs on the air now—shows that deconstruct love in a competitive arena, and are filmed in a documentary "reality" style, such as the long-running "The Bachelor," and "The Bachelorette." "The Bachelor" incorporates "rose ceremonies" into its elimination rites, a symbol of Aphrodite. What does it say about our culture that these shows are so popular? Why do we make love a game? What happens when Hermes plays hardball in Aphrodite's arena? This essay was originally titled "Love Might Hurt, But We Still Like to Watch" and published in The Los Angeles Times on August 8, 2000, p. F3.)

Three shows test struggling couples' devotion, and solid ratings suggest that romantic misery loves company. Are you single? Committed? Not sure?

Television is there for you—with an array of edgy relationship shows that capitalize on romantic waffling. "Change of Heart," "Blind Date" and "Friends or Lovers" are among the programs currently on the air that explore dating, mating and a new ingredient—ambivalence.

Case in point: the national relationship show leader, "Change of Heart." Every episode features a young couple unsure if they want to stay together. Separately, they go out for one night with someone else, testing their commitment level. The pair report on their blind dates before a live audience, mediated by host Chris Jagger. They also reveal the pros and cons about their coupling with shocking candor.

The blind dates are interviewed in the mix as well. Each installment's built-in tension comes with the question: Will the couple work it out or decide to split up? In the final moments, the girl and guy hold up separate cards that announce: "Stay Together" or "Change of Heart." Sometimes, the pain of the discarded partner is visible when the "Change" card appears; sometimes, a decision to stay together elicits derisive groans from the studio audience.

Scott St. John, "Change of Heart's" creator and executive producer, recognizes why the audience relates to the genre. "With the proliferation of cameras and technology and the number of channels we have, we've reduced what's important enough to cover in television down to its most basic level: It's humanity."

According to Nielsen Media Research, season to date, the syndicated "Change of Heart" especially resonates with Los Angeles women. In its late-night slot, it's No. 1 with females 18 to 34 years old, and No. 2 among females 18 to 49, just barely behind "The Tonight Show." Roughly 2.6 million viewers nationally tune in to watch the show each night.

"Blind Date," the second-ranked relationship show with about 2 million viewers nationwide, hosted by Roger Lodge, also showcases attraction and ambivalence. Two people are videotaped on a blind date: pop culture reality deconstructed with editorial comments.

After the date ends, the guy and gal separately confess their real feelings about the outing to the camera. Will they have another date, or was one encounter enough? Once again, the climactic draw is the choice between sticking it out with a potential partner or calling it kaput.

USA Network's "Friends or Lovers," moderated by Andi Matheny, debuted in March, and explores relationship ambiguity with an added component. The setup: One pal doubts the trustworthiness of the other's lover. The intervening friend tries to sour the other's love relationship by revealing a secret. The romantic partner in question eventually takes the stage, joining the fray.

As part of the proceedings, the lover may "take the floor" to plead his or her version of the story, or to ask for forgiveness. In the end, the one in the relationship must choose whom to invite for a tropical vacation: the friend or the lover. If the lover is rejected, the implication is clear: the relationship is on the rocks.

The appeal of these shows for viewers, according to Dr. Tom Lewis, assistant clinical professor of psychiatry at the UC San Francisco School of Medicine and co-author of the book "A General Theory of Love," can be linked to a series of sociopsychological factors.

"As family and community ties weaken, as more and more marriages dissolve, as many in our society become lonelier and isolated, people are left with a tremendous hunger for human connection," he says. "At the same time, they're baffled about how to get the love they want and need. And so it's satisfying for them to watch people on TV fighting the same fight."

Some therapists suggest that these TV programs are actually healthy, authentic reflections of our twenty-first century struggles with romantic commitment. Daphne Rose Kingma, relationship expert, psychotherapist and author of "The Future of Love," says: "In the last decades—in the self-help century—there's been a myth that if you worked at a relationship hard enough, if you figured yourself out psychologically and figured out the differences between men and women, you could have a perfect relationship. But now we're getting a chance to see our ambivalence about relationships and how truly complex they really are."

Kathryn Brown, psychotherapist and chair of the Counseling Psychology Program at Pacifica Graduate Institute, Carpinteria, believes that these new relationship shows—which test relationships, explore commitment quandries and ambivalence—perform a healing function for our culture.

"People who go on these shows are willing to represent something in the collective," Brown says. "If it touches this many people, then it needs to be spoken out loud so that people can get in touch with their own ambiguities or questions in a safe way."

Critics of the new relationship shows categorize them as sensational "trash TV" and question their veracity.

St. John says that on "Change of Heart" the relationships and the situations are real. "This is a show that asks a lot of the people that come on it, frankly. We're dealing with real couples in real situations, and there have been times when we get ready the day before a taping—everyone's gone on their dates, we've found out all the things we've wanted to find out—and they break up the night before. Maybe they start talking to one another. One of them hears that their partner had a great date. They say, 'I'm not coming on the show.' That happens to us."

"Friends or Lovers" host Matheny agrees. "They certainly reflect the culture as it is...I do notice that the majority of women on our show are strong and have dumped boyfriends on a dime when they've learned of unacceptable behavior."

Just how well do the results that play out on the shows match the real world? On "Change of Heart," about fifty percent of the couples decide to stay together—about the same percentage for current marriages that last.

12) End Times: Old Problem, New Myth

(Note: The "end times" have been discussed frequently in the early years of the twenty-first century, both in politics and pop culture; two examples from pop culture are the film "2012," and the apocalyptic prophecies interpreted [or misinterpreted, as many have pointed out] from the ancient Mayan calendar. In this essay, originally published in 1999, many of the observations about "end times" are still valid, especially the history of the issue as a mythological one. Replace "Y2K" with "2012" as the latest iteration of the myth of the Apocalypse? "Old Problem, New Myth: Y2K Hype Latest Manifestation of Humanity's Resistance to Change" was originally published in The Los Angeles Daily News, Viewpoint, Sunday, June 20, 1999, p. 3.)

Will civilization end as we change millenniums? No, but something special is going one. We've witnessed the birth of a new cultural myth. The Y2K bug is a very real technological problem, but the wild speculation that's part of Y2K cybermythology is a psychological reaction. Y2K, the cybermyth, has developed into the most recent incarnation of *fin de siècle* or millennium doomsday tales that manifest periodically throughout history. This time, television and Internet media have helped to sensationalize and promote its portent.

The growing Y2K pandemonium carries the weight of centuries of past dire predictions. Y2K is no longer just an imminent computer malfunction; it becomes an international symbol of technology's dominance over man. Since this glitch will occur as we're changing millenniums—giving it mythological resonance—a rational response, for many, has been replaced by an imaginary one. It's time to calm down and separate the technical problem from its cybermyth counterpart.

Since ancient times, visionaries have asserted that the world was coming to an end. Sacred American Indian tales forecast that a great fire or battle would destroy the world. Iranian prophet Zoroaster Spitama, who lived in the seventh and six centuries B.C., predicted a "Last Judgment" around 2200. His ideas influenced Judaism, Christianity, and Islam. The Hebrew seer Daniel, circa 605-562 B.C., contributed the notion of individual resurrection through the process of apocalypse in the Book of Daniel. The time period of one thousand years—the millennium—is first linked to an apocalypse in the New Testament in John's Book of Revelation, written somewhere between 68 and 95 A.D.

The end of the first millennium inspired elaborate interpretations of impending doom, especially among Europeans. Italian abbot Joachim of Fiore (1135–1202) was the first to connect apocalyptic patterns in the Old and New Testaments. During the Enlightenment, allusions to a new dawn began to manifest in political rhetoric.

America has produced its own unique set of millenarian mystics, including New England farmer William Miller, who spawned a major movement in the 1840s. When the world did not end in 1843, as Miller predicted, his fifty thousand supporters were lampooned in the press; several Millerites then founded other campaigns, including the Seventh-day Adventist Church and the Kellogg brothers' holistic health crusade.

In this country, David Koresh's compound in Waco, Texas, and the Heaven's Gate assembly near San Diego are more recent examples of American millenarianism. Y2K has grown into the latest vision of apocalypse to fascinate the American psyche.

In über-techno 1999, Y2K—in addition to historical baggage—has its own psychological implications. Just the term, "Y2K," promotes the vitality of the virtual world. In a subtle way, those three simple digits imply a victory of technology over language. The cumbersome, human phrase "the year two thousand" has been replaced by the more impersonal, computer-codified Y2K. It embodies the problem. Familiar phrasing is outdated; new technospeak reigns supreme. This contributes to Y2K's powerful emblematic mystique at an unconscious level—out with the old words and in with the new chips.

The various numeric associations of Y2K are also psychically provocative. What is it about 999s changing to 000s that scares us? At a basically symbolic level, there is a resonance of nihilism connected to the shift. Nine suggests abundance; zero registers absence. Fear of nothingness is related to fear of death; it could merely be the death of an era that we're witnessing, but we can't be sure.

Finally, there is uncertainty about the logistics of Y2K. When does the new millennium really start? It might begin Jan. 1, 2000, or in Arthur C. Clarke's *2001*—another date with stark futuristic resonance. Confusion about the next millennium's go date has added to Y2K's mythic reverberations.

The Y2K bug might manifest in late 1999, the psychological effect of allowing computer glitches to mark the inception date of the new millennium makes us feel even more helpless. The notion of remaining in a limbo state for 12-16 months ("Are we there yet?") while computers are updated worldwide is even less empowering. The resulting implication is that Y2K can't be defined or controlled. No one knows when it really begins. No one knows how or when the Y2K bug will end. It feels bigger than we are.

Add up all the factors—the historical legacies, the psychological effects, the logistical uncertainties, the expansive scope—and Y2K begins to feel mysterious, numinous, and ominous.

The advent of the new millennium is like the ultimate New Year's resolution: It forces a reckoning ritual, a look in the mirror to see we really are, and where we hope to be. *Fin de siècle*/millennium mythologies have long been popular with humans because, collectively, we need a reason to take stock of where we stand. What are our achievements as a society? What are our failings as a culture? Implied in a communal reckoning is a chance for change, an opportunity for renewal: We can make things better. Within the notion of apocalypse, there are always seeds of hope for healing and regeneration.

The current Y2K panic, centered on catastrophic endings, should be replaced by an attitudinal shift to composed, symbolic beginnings. The Y2K computer bug is real. But even if there are major temporary disruptions caused by computer glitches, the world is not going to end.

We're living in an extraordinary time, the ending of one millennium and the beginning of a new one. Some of us are responding anxiously to this era's end and blaming it on the Y2K bug. Our collective, cultural response to this epochal shift must be separated from the secondary computer problems occurring concomitantly. As long as we distinguish the Y2K doomsday cybermyth from its technical reality, we can purposefully respond to both, and begin the millennium with a new understanding.

13) Revolution and the *I Ching:*
A Meditation on Hexagram 49

(Note: This essay was originally published in Mythopoetry Scholar, Volume Three: "Revolution." January 2, 2012, with the title "Revolution and the I Ching: Hexagram 49 Reflections." It was published with an image I drew of this hexagram.)

A legendary, imprisoned king who leads a revolt. Fire in the middle of a lake. The hide of a yellow ox. A "proper day." Talk of revolution that circles three times. A tiger. A panther. These are the key images of Hexagram Forty-Nine of *The I Ching* or *Book of Changes.*[93] Hexagram Forty-Nine[94] is connected to the concept of animal moltings; as a symbol, it embodies socio-political revolution, personal transformation, and ever-shifting life cycles.

The *I Ching* is a timeless text that resonates through the ages; it is a unique, interactive repository of Chinese history, philosophy, religion, psychology, mythology and ethics. When used as a divination system, the *I Ching* offers one million possible answers.[95] It is probably the oldest of the *Five Classics* of Chinese literature, and, as J.J. Clarke writes in *Jung and Eastern Thought*, "could justifiably be described as one of the most important books in the world's literature."[96]

Edward L. Shaughnessy notes in his 1998 *I Ching: The Classic of Changes*: "For the last two thousand and more years, the *Yijing (I Ching)* or *Classic of Changes* has been, with the Bible, the most read and commented on work in all of world literature."[97]

The forty-ninth hexagram, illustrated here, is named "Ko /Revolution (Molting)" in the 1950 Richard Wilhelm-Cary F. Barnes translation.[98] It is named "Ge—Abolishing the Old" in the 1998 Alfred Huang Taoist translation.[99]

In order to unpack the significance of this hexagram as related to revolution, I'll begin with a brief look at the *I Ching*'s origin. Then, I'll reflect on the hexagram's key images and its changing lines. My intention here is not to reduce the sacred *I Ching* text to symbolic value only, but rather to try to understand the concept of "revolution" through this hexagram's prominent archetypal insights.[100]

ORIGIN

Experts cannot pinpoint the exact date of the *I Ching*'s creation, and traditionally, its authorship is credited to early Chinese culture heroes. However, in recent scholarship, it is viewed as "an accretion of Western Zhou divinatory concepts."[101]

In *Understanding the I Ching: The History and Use of the World's Most Ancient System of Divination*, Tom Riseman details its traditional heritage: "The legendary sage Fu Hsi is credited with the discovery of the eight basic trigrams—although their names are probably not even Chinese, which puts their origin somewhat vaguely between 25,000 and 5,000 years ago."[102]

According to legend, King Wen of the Zhou Dynasty, unfairly imprisoned around 1150 B.C.E., is said to have expanded the initial eight trigrams to sixty four six-line hexagrams and to have created commentaries about each symbol. The ruler accomplished this while serving a long jail sentence—adding a sense of spiritual irony to the *I Ching*'s legacy.[103]

Some sources attribute the *I Ching* meditations *The Ten Wings* [*Shi Yi*] to King Wen's hand; others assign authorship to Confucius.

It was Confucius who brought the book into, as Shaughnessey writes, "prominent philosophical significance."[104] But some scholars doubt that Confucius actually wrote any of it at all; textual evidence indicates he did not.[105] Riseman connects Confucius and Taoism to the development of the *Book of Changes*: "It was he [Confucius] who first named the *I Ching* 'The Changes' and he produced study after study of it. Taoism is inseparable from the philosophy of the *I Ching*. It is based on the complimentary yet antagonistic principles of *yin* and *yang*, both creating and destroying each other by the ceaseless rearrangements of their relationship."[106]

In the eleventh and twelfth centuries, four leading figures of the Sung *culterati* chose the *I Ching* as a vehicle to help transform Chinese intellectual life.[107] In *Sung Dynasty Uses of the I Ching*, authors Kidder Smith, Jr., Peter K. Bol, Joseph A. Adler, and Don J. Wyatt write about perceptions of the *I Ching's* multivalence during the Sung dynasty. It functioned "as a work of culture that links men to many things: to the mind of sages, to nature and universal process, and thus to the ground of value and the roots of morality."[108]

Archaeological discoveries in the twentieth century contributed to further historical understanding of the *I Ching*. New revelations about the tools used in the divination process include turtle shells or bones bearing *I Ching* questions found at Anyang, Henan, the last capital of the Shang dynasty, circa 1600–1045 B.C.E.[109]

The *I Ching* was used as a model for China's—and the world's—first civil service. Riseman notes that Chiang Kai-Shek "extolled the *I Ching* as an oracle and a basis of the 'Ultimate

Virtues' of the Chinese."[110] It was considered a strategic battle primer until World War II, when it fell into disuse. Mao Tse-Tung consulted the *I Ching* as a tactical guide to prepare for the battles of the Long March.[111]

In the nineteenth and twentieth centuries, the use of the *Book of Changes* expanded globally, employed by such diverse groups as fortune-tellers and stock market analysts,[112] as its vatic function was explored (and some would say exploited) in the West. New, accessible English translations of the *I Ching* were published in the twentieth century. Translation is important to the worldwide impact of the *I Ching*; scholars debate the value and bias of many of the most famous translations in English, including the Richard Wilhelm-Cary F. Barnes version—from Chinese to German to English—favored by C. G. Jung.[113]

Jung's interest in the *I Ching*—and it was not a casual one—began in 1920. He writes in *Memories, Dreams, Reflections*: "One summer in Bollingen I resolved to make an all-out attack on the riddle of this book…I would sit for hours on the ground beneath the hundred year-old pear tree, the *I Ching* beside me, practicing the technique by referring the resultant oracles to one another in an interplay of questions and answers. All sorts of undeniably remarkable results emerged—meaningful connections with my own thought processes which I could not explain to myself."[114] Frank McFlynn writes in *Carl Gustav Jung* that by 1931 Jung had "concluded that the *I Ching* was simply his own theory of dreams expressed in different language."[115] The *I Ching* was foundational to Jung's theories of synchronicity and the unconscious.[116]

It is especially relevant to an exploration of revolution that a key figure mentioned in *I Ching* tradition and text, King Wen, was revered for leading a revolt against the ruling Shang Dynasty; after Wen's death his victorious son founded the Zhou Dynasty.[117]

HEXAGRAM 49

And what does the specific hexagram itself reveal about revolution? There is an ordered, cosmic sequence to the *I Ching*. In the Wilhelm-Barnes translation, Hexagram 48 is named "Ching—The Well."[118] Hexagram 48 is named "Jing—Replenishing" in the Huang translation.[119] After filling the well or replenishment, it is time to clear out the old ways and make room for the new; thus, Hexagram 49 is "Ge—Abolishing the Old."[120]

Huang writes that "Ge" once meant "the hide of the animal."[121] The hide or skin goes through a process in tanning, thus transforming it. Later, the meaning of "Ge" broadened to include "change," improvement, and innovation. The two trigrams that make up this hexagram are "Dui (Lake—Above)" and "Li (Fire—Below)." From an archetypal perspective, these trigrams are characterized as two quarreling sisters in the same home—who eventually marry into other families, starting anew. Huang notes: "Water and fire overcome each other. This phenomenon suggests a picture of revolution—abolishing the old."[122] Huang cites the "Confucius' Commentary" on the Decision of Hexagram 49: "'Heaven and Earth abolish the old and bring about the new, then the four seasons complete their changes. Tang and Wu[123]...brought about the new. They obeyed the will of Heaven in accord with the wishes of the people. The time and meaning of abolishing the old is truly great!'"[124] Here, there is praise for two legendary revolutionary leaders who lead the people to "the new"; guidance of the people is seen as inspired by the celestial: "the will of Heaven."

The first image in the hexagram's commentary is "Fire in the Midst of a Lake."[125] This is the symbol of revolution, and a cautionary note is included: one must be steadfast, observe the heavens and the shift of seasons. Of the hexagram's significance, the Huang translation reads: "It is progress, an improvement.

Revolution does not happen by accident. There is always a reason. One can never create a revolution."[126]

An *I Ching* hexagram is created and read from the bottom line upwards.[127] The six changing lines of Hexagram 49 provide further insights into the stages of revolution. To fully comprehend a hexagram's changing lines and the individual significance of each one, there are important correspondences to yin and yang lines and other valuable trigram correlatives that should be understood.[128] Here, however, I will limit my reflections to the changing lines and their cumulative key symbols linked to the concept of revolution.

1) Changing Line One refers to being tied or bound to the hide or skin of a yellow ox.[129] This image shows that the revolution is just beginning, in a nascent form. The revolution needs to coalesce; participants must bond before further action may be taken. Huang identifies the yellow ox as an Earth-related image.[130] The cow is perceived as a sign of fertility; the movement has potential but cannot succeed without preparations.

2) Changing Line Two highlights: "Proper Day." This means: Act now. Doing so will ensure good fortune and social transformation. The revolution begins; success is promised. Huang's interpretation connects light's "brilliance" to the timing of the right day.[131]

3) Changing Line Three cautions against moving forward too quickly in the revolution. This is premature and will bring misfortune. The revolution's purpose must be explained three times[132]—just as King Wu did during "the revolution against the Tyrant of Shang."[133] Legge writes that the third line "has passed the centre of Sun and is on its outward verge."[134] If sincerity of purpose is

expressed repeatedly, the revolution may be saved, however. All is not lost.

4) Changing Line Four is about the termination of any regrets related to the revolution. Once the revolution's purpose is clearly communicated, remorse about ensuing transformation and the revolution process will dissolve. Sincerity and truth are key here.

5) Changing Line Five says: "Great person/Changes like a tiger."[135] In Huang's translation, this line means that the movement's leader must transform herself or himself first (in regards to the new principles sought), thus earning the peoples' trust and respect: "merit is as brilliant and distinct as a tiger's fur."[136] There is no need to seek confirmation of such a revolutionary leader's character with an oracle or a divine sign, because it is obvious to everyone—as visible as a tiger's unique fur pattern. King Wen was thought to be such a leader.

6) Changing Line Six relates to changing like a panther.[137] The revolution has run its course; the social sphere must return to its regular state. The panther's fur was thought to change with the seasons.[138] All good leaders and followers should do the same. Although there will always be some who only change at a superficial level, it is important not to continue to push for further transformation at this juncture. It will not succeed.

REFLECTIONS

The sacred text of the *I Ching's* Hexagram 49 contains vibrant insights about the organic nature of revolution and its sequential phases. The hexagram shows that primal forces are at great odds in a revolution's beginning, as in the image of two quarreling, competing sisters whose interests finally diverge. The fire in the middle of a lake helps us to visualize how revolution exists: its powerful, crackling flames are reflected in the water that surrounds it; its light and smoke touch the celestial plane. No revolution starts without a reason; you cannot decide to create a social or political movement. It happens organically. Timing is part of a revolution's success. A good leader must "change" herself or himself first: personal transformation is part of the political, as is shown through the figure of King Wen.

The phases (including pitfalls) of a revolution and its process are embodied in Hexagram 49. Once a revolution is birthed, it must be "bound with the hide of a yellow ox," in order to have laid the foundations necessary for it to proceed successfully, such as commitment and allegiance. The revolution will launch on the "proper day," a time of brilliance. A setback: The purpose of the revolution may be explained "three times," as in a charm or spell. It is in threes that magic happens in fairy and folk tales. Do not proceed until the goals are clearly articulated, repeated, circulated. Regret will vanish when the goals are clear. A great leader changes like a tiger whose stripes are obvious even from afar; her or his sincerity is visible to all. When the revolution ends, everyone must change—this time, like the panther. Eras evolve; a new stability must come after revolution. Hexagram 49 infers that revolution has the ability to "enlighten," since it is "brilliant" on its "proper day," and has an elemental fire association.

The *I Ching* is called *Book of Changes*; Hexagram 49 describes the specific changes in "Revolution," whose purpose is "to establish the new. The new should be better than the old."[139] Legge's translation says revolution "is believed in only after it has been accomplished. There will be great progress and success. Advantage will come from being firm and correct."

[93] The standard English translation of *I Ching* is *Book of Changes*. It is the practice of scholars writing in English to use the Chinese title and its English translation interchangeably. See, for example, Harold Coward in *Jung and Eastern Thought*. Eds. Richard D. Mann and Jean B. Mann. Albany: State U of New York Press, 1985, p. 90. The *I Ching* is also referred to as the *Classic of Changes*.

[94] For an image of Hexagram 49, please visit: http://en.wikipedia.org/wiki/File:Iching-hexagram-49.svg.

[95] Beebe, John. "The Influences of the *I Ching*: A Symposium Moderated by John Beebe, Opening Remarks." The *I Ching*: East and West. Jung Institute, San Francisco, California. 17 Oct. 1998.

[96] Clarke, J.J. *Jung and Eastern Thought: A Dialogue With The Orient*. New York: Routledge, 1994, p. 89.

[97] Shaughnessey, Edward L. *The I Ching: The Classic of Changes*. Trans. and commentary. New York: Ballantine, 1998, p. 1.

[98] *The I Ching or Book of Changes*. The Richard Wilhelm Translation in English by Cary F. Baynes. Bollingen Series, XIX. Princeton: Princeton UP, 1950, p. 189.

[99] Huang, Alfred. *The Complete Translation I Ching: Tenth Anniversary Edition*. Rochester, VT, 1998/2010.

[100] Note: There are many significant, complex issues related to the sacred *I Ching* text that are beyond the intended scope of this essay.

[101] "*I Ching*." Wikipedia. http://en.wikipedia.org/wiki/I_Ching#cite_note-7 15 December 2011.

[102] Riseman, Tom. *Understanding the I Ching: The History and Use of the World's Most Ancient System of Divination*. North Hamptonshire, England: Aquarian, 1980., p. 8.

[103] Some accounts say King Wen was imprisoned for eleven years. Huang writes that it was seven years (p. 502). King Wen is revered today as a Chinese hero. He died before the defeat of the Shang dynasty, but his son King Wu defeated them at the battle of Muye in 1045 B.C.E., thus establishing the Zhou Dynasty (Shaughnessy, p. 4).

[104] Shaughnessey, p. 2.

[105] *I Ching*." Wikipedia. http://en.wikipedia.org/wiki/I_Ching#cite_note-Balkin-5. 15 December 2011.

[106] Riseman, pps. 8-9.

[107] The four were: Su Shih, Shao Yung, Ch'eng I and Chu Hsi. Kidder Smith, Jr., Peter K. Bol, Joseph A. Adler, and Don J. Wyatt. *Sung Dynasty Uses of the I Ching*. Princeton, Princeton UP, 1990, p. 3.

[108] Smith et al., p. 206.

[109] Shaughnessey, p. 2.

[110] Riseman, p. 9.
[111] Riseman, p. 9.
[112] Riseman, p. 10. See, for example, the many books on the *I Ching* and business/commercial strategies.
[113] Jung himself writes in 1949: "May not the old text be corrupt? Is Wilhelm's translation accurate?" From "Foreword." *The I Ching or Book of Changes*. The Richard Wilhelm Translation in English by Cary F. Baynes. Bollingen Series, XIX. Princeton: Princeton UP, 1950, p. xxxiii. [Note: My essay, too, is from a Western perspective/bias; I read the *I Ching* in English.]
[114] Jung, C.G. *Memories, Dreams Reflections*. Ed. Aniela Jaffe. New York: Vintage, 1961, p. 373.
[115] McFlynn, Frank. *Carl Gustav Jung*. New York: St. Martin's Press.1996, p. 405.
[116] For more on this, see Coward, pps. 42-43. Also, Jung's "Foreward" to *The I Ching or Book of Changes* [1950], pps. xxi-xxxix, and Jung's work *Synchronicity: An Acausal Connecting Principle*. Trans. R.F.C. Hull. Bollingen Series XX. Princeton: Princeton, UP. 1960.
[117] Shaughnessy, p. 4.
[118] Wilhelm-Barnes, p. 185.
[119] In James Legge's 1882 *I Ching* English translation, which precedes the 1950 Wilhelm-Barnes translation, it is named "Ko." To compare Legge's 1892 translation (in the public domain) to aspects of Huang's "Ge" 1998 translation discussed below, see http://www.sacred-texts.com/ich/ic49.htm.
[120] Huang, p. 389.
[121] Huang, p. 389.
[122] Huang, p. 389.
[123] This refers to King Tan , who overthrew the Xia dynasty and founded the Shang dynasty, and King Wu, son of Wen, who established the Zhou dynasty. Huang, p. 393.
[124] Huang, p. 389.
[125] Huang, p. 391.
[126] Huang, p. 391.
[127] "Hexagram." Wikipedia.org. 3 Dec. 2011. http://en.wikipedia.org/wiki/Hexagram_(I_Ching).
[128] See, for example, Huang, pps. 394–396.
[129] Huang, p. 394. This imagery is in Legge's and Wilhelm-Barnes' translations.
[130] Huang, p. 394.
[131] Huang, p. 394.

[132] "Three times" is in Legge's and Wilhelm-Barnes' translations.
[133] Huang, p. 394.
[134] James Legge translation, http://www.sacred-texts.com/ich/ic49.htm.
[135] Huang, p. 392. The tiger imagery is in Legge's and Wilhelm-Barnes' translations.
[136] Huang, p. 395.
[137] Huang, p. 392. The panther imagery is in Legge's and Wilhelm-Barnes' translations.
[138] Huang, p. 395.
[139] Huang, p. 392.

14) The Trickster and the President

(Note: Originally published with the headline "Clinton's Transformation Into a Mythical Trickster" on February 7, 1999, in The Los Angeles Times, on pages M2 and M6. The essay was published five days before the Senate acquitted President Clinton on charges of perjury and obstruction of justice.)

President Bill Clinton's unwavering popularity continues to stun political analysts. Nothing seems to lower his poll numbers. In spite of the House managers' extensive case and the Senate trial machinations, Clinton's job approval ratings keep improving.

Ironically, it is, perhaps, the Republicans who have most helped Clinton's poll numbers. Because of their prolonged partisan pursuit of the president, Clinton virtually has become a symbol of America's collective conscience. The GOP broadened the scope of Clinton's story into the realm of mythology. They have made him a modern incarnation of the Trickster, a universal archetype that appears in the mythology of virtually every culture. Trickster is the sly underdog, known for his lying, lascivious ways. Caught in his own dance of deception, Trickster's deeds nonetheless often produce positive results.

Trickster is a recurring figure in the sacred tales of people all over the world. Coyote is one incarnation in North America; Spider is another Trickster figure from Africa. Monkey King from China, Fox from South America and Hermes from a Greek pantheon are all embodiments of the Trickster. Revered as a hero, this lowly creature outwits formidable enemies against all odds. Is it part of the human psyche to root for the sneaky underdog? The fact that Trickster exists in mythologies from five continents—the Americas, Africa, Asia and Europe—indicates a universal affinity for the character.

Trickster has the ability to affect his people through his adventures. As a creator-culture-hero transformer, the rascal works through lies and the occasional evil deed. Yet, his intrigues frequently have altruistic outcomes, obtained through twisted schemes. An entire group may benefit from Trickster's wily ways.

For example, Coyote's guile brought water to the world, according to an American Indian tale. Coyote found a deer rib that resembled a giant shell. He traded the phony shell to the frog people, who had dammed all the water, for the chance to drink. Pretending to drink, Coyote dug a hole in the dam, which collapsed and sent water rushing into the dry valleys below. Substitute Clinton for Coyote, and the Republicans for the frog people, and you get one part of Clinton's appeal.

There is a duality to Trickster's nature, a paradoxical mix of bawdiness and holiness. Some of his tales are amusing, even erotic. Notorious for his sex appeal, Trickster often woos many women at the same time, which gets him into trouble. Many North American tales have a moral fabric, to show children what not to do. Often sacred narratives feature a divine, holy Trickster, as in the African Dahomey mythology of Legba. Some American Indian tribes united the sacred and profane nature of the archetype.

In recent pop culture, the cartoon character Wile E. Coyote is a twentieth century American manifestation of the Trickster archetype. The label "Tricky Dick," given to President Richard M. Nixon, is another American cultural allusion to the presence of Trickster. "Slick Willie," Clinton's perjorative nickname, is a more recent invocation of the Trickster symbol.

Clinton's current travails function in a similar way to Trickster tales. Kenneth W. Starr, the independent counsel, cast Clinton firmly in the profane Trickster role, via the graphic sexual content included in the evidentiary materials released in 1998. The House managers have promoted this image through their dogged prosecutorial strategy, tarnishing the president's character with endless inferences of illegality and immorality.

The GOP has activated several functions of the Trickster myth. Though they were implored not to debase the House, the Senate and the American public with explicit allegations, GOP leaders structured their case to feature sexual content. By appearing partisan, they've made Clinton an underdog. Republicans triggered a collective American psychological response that works in Clinton's favor.

The state of the Clinton presidency dominates our culture. The daily news coverage on television and in print, the constant jokes and the flashy Internet gossip via online magazines and Web sites—all promote this event as national ritual. Networks ran special segments on what to tell children. Then there's the endless assessment of public opinion. Clearly, poll results suggest that most Americans are appalled by Clinton's weakness, but accept him as leader for the remainder of his elected term.

The response of the American public resonates with the classical psychological function of the Trickster archetype, an embodiment of both the profane and the sacred in our leader—and our collective acknowledgement of it in ourselves. The current crisis, forcing a national reconciling of policy, morality and the reality of desire gives Americans a platform to examine their own humanity. It allows voters to relate to Clinton at a deeper level than most ever expected: a fragile, human one.

Without the Republicans' prolonged emphasis on graphic sexual detail and their accusations of deception, Clinton might have been permanently reviled. But the GOP's strategy has backfired;

they have transformed Clinton into a mythic archetype. Will another side of the Trickster archetype appear? It's worth remembering that in his American Indian tales, Trickster, after meeting his demise, always miraculously revives for another adventure. And Clinton's other nickname is "the Comeback Kid."

15) Hero Worship and the Academy Awards

(*Note: Parts of this were published in the 2004 Conference Proceedings for "The Image of the Hero in Literature, Media, and Society," Society for the Interdisciplinary Study of Social Imagery [SISSI]. Conference Dates: March 18-20, 2004. Colorado Springs, Colorado. Presented paper: "Oscar Exemplars: Toward an Exploration of Current Heroes, Hero Worship, and the Academy Awards."*)

"If you want a sense of what America is like, you'll watch the Oscars."
—Gil Cates, 2006[140]

On Oscar Night, millions of people worldwide tune in to the glitzy, three hour (or longer) awards show hosted by a star or stars, where Tinseltown's brightest shine. Why do so many people watch? Because it is a mimetic reflection of our culture and of the human psyche—a replay of the key images and characters that have fascinated us for the past year.

To put it another way: the Academy Awards are on an archetypal plane; the huge cinema screen elevates films and film stars to a "larger-than-life" mythic realm. One night a year, we can see our celluloid gods and goddesses in their "civilian" clothes of *haute couture* along side that sleek, golden Oscar statuette, an otherworldly cultural icon in its own right, a symbol of the "best." As Oscars are handed out, we can review, *en masse*—as a collective annual ritual—the central imaginary figures and motifs featured in American pop culture for the past twelve months.

The Best Picture category showcases the main characters, images and stories that have fascinated our psyches for the last year; these films offer compelling reflections of our emotional, psychological, and spiritual states. The ceremony itself puts focus on some of our favorite cinematic male and female actor-heroes by the very nature of the competition. There are some correlatives between hero worship in ancient Greece and "modern" hero worship promoted by the film industry and the Academy Awards ceremony.

BRIEF HISTORY OF HERO WORSHIP

The etymology of "hero" derives from the Latin and Greek *heros*. According to the *Oxford English Dictionary Online*, "Hero" was a "name given (as in Homer) to men of superhuman strength, courage, or ability, favoured by the gods; at a later time regarded as intermediate between gods and men, and immortals" ("Hero"). The concept of heroes as "demi-gods" was a peculiarity of Greek religion for which there are few parallels, according to Walter Burkert in *Greek Religions* (203).

In ancient times, the Greek notion of hero was related to service of others, to physical challenges, and to extraordinary deeds of altruism and sacrifice; Burkert states that heroism was especially celebrated in epic poetry as connected to the development of the Greek *polis* (204). In ancient Greece, as recognition for their service, heroes received special burials. According to Sarah Pomeroy, Stanley Burstein, Walter Donlan, and Jennifer Tolbert Roberts in *Ancient Greece: A Political, Social and Cultural History,* a hero who died was memorialized with tomb rites; thus, the death of a champion/heroine was honored with a rebirth of sorts—the formation of a cult (79). In 750 B.C.E., there was a revival of interest in Greek hero worship. In the eighth century B.C.E., evidence shows that new shrines appeared in honor of legendary figures, like Agamemnon or Helen. According to Pomeroy *et al*: "The impetus behind hero cults was the belief that the great men and women of the Heroic Age had power in death to protect and to help people" (79). There was also a familial-financial component to hero/heroine cults. Many wealthy clans in Athens began to claim ancestral ties to mythic archetypes; these archetypes were considered powerful enough to protect the living. There is also evidence that the connection to local heroes was highly prized: "...Founding ancestors might naturally receive heroic honors" (Burkert 204).

Where did "hero worship" take place? How was it ritualized? Jennifer Larson, in *Greek Heroine Cults*, says that death of the hero is the focal point of a hero-narrative and that the tomb was always the focal point for the cult (9). This localizes hero worship, so that the worship ritual is regionalized and community-specific. Occasionally, however, Larson notes that a hero could be worshipped away from the tomb if a hero became very popular and was raised to a more divine status, such as the archetype of Heracles.

Burial inside city walls or besides city gates, where the hero could protect the city, were the most significant locations for tombs, and an indication of high status and prestige (Larson 9). Burkert points out that "a hero cult involves setting apart one particular grave, known as a *heroon*, from other burials by marking off a special precinct, by bringing sacrifices and votive gifts, and occasionally by building a special grave monument" (203). The rituals were: "attended by blood sacrifices, food offerings, and libations" and "feastings of the living" (Burkert 205). Burkert also says that hero worship was ultimately an expression of the collective, of "group solidarity" (204).

MODERN MOVIES AND HERO WORSHIP

Are modern movie theatres similar to ancient crypts? Certainly some aspects of the darkened theatre, where silence is prized, evoke comparisons to sacred burial chambers. Enjoying popcorn and drinking soft drinks may not be exactly the same thing as "food offerings, libations" and "feastings." But the act of eating in the dark, while concentrating on a hero-driven narrative with life and death as key points of the plot, is in some ways a comparable activity when viewed from a ritual perspective. Watching movies in a theatre is done collectively, with others around you; it is a social experience, and viewing films as part of a temporary collective audience may promote "group solidarity" in terms of audience response as well.

Millions of American viewers tune into the Academy Awards broadcast each year; no exact numbers are available for the international viewers, although estimates are as high as one hundred million (Pals). The argument may be made that the Oscars ceremony is a universally-prized, modern annual ritual due to four significant factors:

> I) its connection to modern mythos and drama (it serves as a dramatic review—a review of the most popular stories in filmic/dramatic form of each year);

> II) the focus on the drama-within-the-drama (via announcements of winners/ "heroes" in the broadcast). It is its own contest/competition/trial in terms of

dramatic structure; the broadcast itself functions as a "hero machine," by anointing "the best" in each category. There are vast professional and personal benefits extended to those who "win");

III) the emphasis on sartorial status (high fashion style, physically perfect appearance, personal aesthetics) of the actor-hero/actor-heroine (a press-sponsored "deification" of them, thus another tie to hero worship from a cultural standpoint, especially related to the "red carpet" aspect of the event);

IV) a rite, international in scope, that unifies around the Academy Awards ceremony and celebrated movies.

The Oscars ceremony highlights films that mirror images in our fears, our hopes, and our dreams. It could be seen as a significant cultural barometer in terms of what stories and images are seen as "heroic." What is the value of looking at an annual collection of cinematic heroes, as highlighted by the Academy Awards nominees and broadcast? Jean Mitry writes in *The Aesthetics and Psychology of the Cinema:* "In any case, it is not I, as an individual, who identifies with the hero; it is an unfulfilled wish, an ideal Self which I recognize in him" (85).

WORKS CITED

Burkert, Walter. *Greek Religions.* Trans. John Raffan. Cambridge, MA; Harvard UP, 1985.

"Hero." *Oxford English Dictionary Online.* May 22, 2004. <http://dictionary.oed.com/cgi/entry/00105293?query/_&

type=word&querywords=hero&addition=2e&first=1&Max_ 2_show=10&sorts_type=alpha&results_places=1&search_id =+AHP-TQNDL5-1950&hilite=00105293>.

Larson, Jennifer. *Greek Heroine Cults*. Madison, WI: University of Wisconsin Press, 1995.

Mitry, Jean. *The Aesthetics and Psychology of the Cinema*. Trans. Christopher King. Bloomington, IN; Indiana UP, 2000.

Pals, Arthur J. "How Does One Say No To Clint Eastwood?" February 21, 2004. <http://www.rediff.com/cms/print.jsp?docpath=/movies/2004/feb/21oscar.htm> March 15, 2004.

Pomeroy, Sarah, Stanley M. Burstein, Walter Donlan, and Jennifer Tobert Roberts. *Ancient Greece: A Political, Social and Cultural History*. Oxford: Oxford University Press, 1999.

---

[140] http://www.tvweek.com/blogs/tvbizwire/2011/11/longtime-producer-of-the-oscar.php.

16) Movies and Creation Myth—*2001: A Space Odyssey*

(*Note:* My review of "2001: A Space Odyssey" was originally published on the C.G. Jung Page [cgjung.org] in January 2001. I suggest that viewing this film at the beginning of each year may be a useful personal ritual. I share observations about creation myth, Apollo, and the Roman god Janus.)

"2001: A Space Odyssey." 1968. Released by MGM. Written by Arthur C. Clarke and Stanley Kubrick; based on "The Sentinel," by Arthur C. Clarke. Directed and Produced by Stanley Kubrick. Music by Aram Khachaturyan, György Ligeti, Richard Strauss and Johann Strauss. Cinematography by John Alcott (additional photography), Geoffrey Unsworth. Stanley Kubrick was also special photographic effects designer and director. Kubrick won an Academy Award for these special effects. Starring Keir Dullea as Dr. David "Dave" Bowman with Douglas Rain (Voice) as HAL 9000. Rated G.

I was a child when "2001: A Space Odyssey" was originally released, and I remember thinking that 2001 seemed so very far away—a date that would surely never arrive. It was the surreal, abstract future. For me, in 1968, trying to imagine the year 2001 was akin to contemplating how many numbers it took to make "infinity." It was headache-inducing, and impossible to do.

2001 has come and gone. And I highly recommend revisiting "2001: A Space Odyssey" to begin a New Year, as a meditation on soul. Filmmaker Stanley Kubrick and writer Arthur C. Clarke's updated examination of creation myths in "2001" is an attempt to grapple with the metaphysical nature of the human experience—the bright lights of the stars and the deep space shadows: ultimately, our spiritual destiny.

Space is a metaphor for the collective psyche. As Joseph Campbell writes of creation myths in *The Inner Reaches of Outer Space*:

"It is an old, old story in mythology: of the Alpha and the Omega that is the ground of all being, to be realized as the beginning and the end of this life. The imagery is necessarily physical and thus apparently of outer space. The inherent connotation is always, however, psychological and metaphysical, which is to say, of inner space" (31).

About myths of the universe, C.G. Jung writes: "Now we know that cosmogonic myths are, at bottom, symbols for the coming of consciousness...The dawn-state corresponds to the unconscious..." (*Aion* 148). And so "2001" begins, after the eerie yet beautiful Overture, with a title that reads "The Dawn of Man." Sunrise breaks as the famous theme song "Also Sprach Zarathustra (Thus Spoke Zarathustra)" by Richard Strauss crescendos. This four-part odyssey begins with the story of primordial apes who radically change from peaceful to violent when a mysterious black monolith appears near them, emitting strange vibrations. After a bloody skirmish, an ape hurls a bone into the air and it morphs into a spaceship. The film's symbolism is direct: It's the future, but don't be fooled. The tools of violence may look different, filmmaker Kubrick warns, but high technology is weaponry all the same.

Suddenly, it's 2000: shuttles dock in space stations as if it's a quotidian occurrence, a mere plane ride. Voice Print Identification is used for security purposes; phone calls are made with cards. Videophones have replaced the old "auditory-only" telephone machines; a father is too busy to attend his young daughter's birthday party. Zero-Gravity toilets are routine; flight attendants serve freeze-dried food as the in-flight meal. Stress pills are dispensed as required.

And through it all, there are images of round orbs, rotating spheres, moving circles and planets. These are symbols of Self. Of round images, Gaston Bachelard observes in *The Poetics of Space*: "I repeat, images of full roundness help us to collect ourselves, permit us to confer an initial constitution on ourselves, and to confirm our being innately, inside" (234). In *Flying Saucers*, Jung says that for the modern psyche, spaceships represent "self": "They are impressive manifestations of totality whose simple, round form portrays the archetype of the self..." (21). Space travel in "2001," then, is a metaphoric quest for an understanding of the complexity of the human soul—who we are, inside out.

In the second part, "2001" follows the life of Dr. Heywood R. Floyd (William Sylvester), of the National Council of Astronauts. There's a mystery on the moon that warrants an official investigation. A strange dark monolith has been unearthed on the American base of Clavius; it was apparently buried 4 million years hence. When approached by space-suited Dr. Floyd and company, the monolith again begins to emit its bizarre siren song.

The next title announces "The Jupiter Mission," eighteen months later: Part Three. We're introduced to Dr. Frank Poole (Gary Lockwood), as he jogs, shadow-boxing, around the spaceship Discovery on a vertical white running track—as if it's a treadmill. Frank wears a black shirt and white shorts. Here, too, the imagery is metaphoric; in spite of all this efficient technology, humankind is still trapped in the same rat race, fighting the shadow; we wear the colors of our inherent duality—the innate struggle with good and evil.

The Jupiter Mission is irregular from the start; its purpose is unclear. Three male crew members are in hibernation via cryogenics to be revived upon arrival. Only Dr. Frank Poole and the mission commander, Dr. David "Dave" Bowman (Keir Dullea), are awake to "man" the mission. In a clever expositional scene, Dave and Frank tape an interview with a BBC 12 reporter explaining what they're doing in deep space—an ironic nod to media influence reaching as far as away as Jupiter. Dave and Frank are able to watch the broadcast as they eat; celestial talus cruises by as the ship blasts towards Jupiter.

At this point we're introduced to the super HAL 9000 computer, portrayed by the voice of Douglas Rain. HAL, an acronym derived from "Heuristic" and "Algorithm," constellates the archetype of Apollo in "2001"; he is the most "reliable computer ever made," "foolproof and incapable of error." Detached, disembodied, and represented physically by a ubiquitous, watchful camera lens that looks like the iris of a human eye or a red orb with a yellow Apollonian sun in the center, HAL "enjoys working with people." He is "constantly occupied" putting himself "to the fullest possible use." HAL runs the entire ship; there is no aspect of the mission that escapes his control. HAL is the nexus to all; human life is at the mercy of technology in "2001."

Karl Kerényi says in the book *Apollo*: "For the Greeks, Apollo was something quite special, more than son of the celestial body, and even more than the mature paternal sun God. Like all the great Olympians, he is, so to speak, the center of the world from which the whole of existence seems to have a different appearance" (44-45). Christine Downing observes that "Apollo represents clarity, coolness, objectivity…" (85). Ginette Paris, in *Pagan Meditations*, credits Apollo with intellectual rigor (17).

On board, Frank and Dave occupy their spare time with video transmissions from Earth and computer chess matches. Like Big Brother, HAL is always watching. But Mission Control, from Earth, reports disturbing news; some of HAL's calculations are wrong. Frank suspects that HAL is malfunctioning; Dave concurs. But before they can disconnect HAL, Kubrick inserts an Intermission and a suspenseful musical "Entre'Acte."

In the second half of the film, HAL kills Frank and the three hibernating crew members. This, too, is part of the Apollonian archetype. Apollo had, as Callimachus notes in the classic Hymn to Apollo, a Lyctian bow and quiver. He was famous for "the strength of an unerring marksman" (Barnard 3). Apollo kills; Downing states in *Gods In Our Midst* that Apollo murders in order to purify, to bring order (89). HAL fears he will be useless after the mission's completion, and thus takes action to ensure he will not be disconnected—that his "consciousness" will stay intact. Kubrick and Clarke's implication is that unbridled Apollonian energy, without the balance of compassion in the mix, can destroy the soul. The recurring motif of violence in "2001" is part of Kubrick and Clarke's meditation on spirituality: will we ever transcend this dark part of our nature? Or is it our eternal downfall?

Filmmaker Kubrick shows an extended sequence of Frank falling through outer space while Dave tries to retrieve his body. Thus Frank becomes a symbol of techno-sacrifice; in an unforgettable image, a dead Poole is held outside the ship's doors in the white robotic arms of a spacepod. The arms reach upwards, offering Frank to the dark universe. Soon afterwards, because of HAL's increasing deterioration, Dave must let Frank fall away into the infinite space void, the sacrifice complete.

A "battle" sequence between HAL and Dave ensues. In a famous monologue, when HAL seemingly speaks from his anima, he says: "Just what do you think you're doing, Dave? Dave, I really think I'm entitled to an answer to that question. I know everything hasn't been quite right with me. But I can assure you now, very confidently, that it's going to be all right again. I feel much better now. I really do. Look, Dave. I can see you're really upset about this. I honestly think you ought to sit down calmly, take a stress pill, and think things over. I know I've made some very poor decisions recently, but I can give you my complete assurance that my work will be back to normal..."

HAL then repeatedly beseeches Dave to stop trying to override his circuitry. But Dave continues to pursue disconnection. Hal implores: "Stop, Dave. I'm afraid." HAL reveals that the real purpose of the Jupiter Mission was to track a transmission that the strange monolith made to the planet Jupiter. HAL's sputtering breakdown also produces significant biographical material: HAL became operational at the main plant in Urbana, Illinois, on January 12, 1992—a reference to Middle America and modern technology with an implied warning: too much technological dependence is dangerous. HAL is American. Regressed in his breakdown to a childlike state, Hal sings his first programming recollection—a song he refers to as "Daisy," more commonly called "A Bicycle Built for Two." But The Discovery is about to become a vehicle for One.

The last title reads: "Jupiter and Beyond the Infinite." HAL's demise coincides with the third return of the dark monolith in "2001," this time near a Jupiter moon. Dave climbs into a spacepod to investigate. The colorful psychedelic light show in the third act of the film represents the final spiritual frontier for Dave, and for the rest of us. No longer in the monochromatic lights and darks, rainbow hues literally explode across the screen, as the pod careens through blinding iridescence. Images from creation mythology abound. Quasars, starbursts, Big Bang nebulae, the Milky Way, plasma, amniotic fluid, fetal imagery: it's all there. The ship is eventually guided by seven flying diamonds above shifting landscapes—shimmering volcanic residue, canyon lands, and deserts.

It all comes to a sudden screeching halt in a surreal white room. In this sequence, Dave, as Everyman, regards himself in a bathroom mirror: facing the Self at last as he rapidly ages. When the monolith appears in his white bedroom, as he feebly lies in bed, it is now a black door, a threshold experience, a gateway to death. But waiting on the other side is a baby in a womb: his rebirth as a "Star-Child." In these last moments of "2001," the monolith represents the presence of Janus, the Roman god of light and dark, of doorways and thresholds, of the heavenly vault, of beginnings: the portal to transcendence.

Kubrick shows, in his beautiful movie, that although the human experience is one of eternal struggle, with the brain at war with the heart, there is always spiritual regeneration. Violence is part of our past, and too often part of our present. Death will chase us—and win. But the collective human spirit will survive, to be born again—naïve and anew—in each subsequent generation, each New Millennium.

Works Cited

Bachelard, Gaston. *The Poetics of Space*. Trans. Colette Gaudin. Dallas: Spring, 1971.

Barnard, Mary. *The Myth of Apollo and Daphne from Ovid to Quevedo: Love, Agon and the Grotesque*. Durham: N.C.: Duke UP, 1987.

Campbell, Joseph. *The Inner Reaches of Outer Space*. N.p.: HarperPerrenial, 1986.

Downing, Christine. *Gods in Our Midst*. New York: Crossroad, 1993.

Jung, C. G. *Aion*: Researches into the Phenomenology of the Self. Trans. R.F.C. Hull. Bollingen Series XX. Princeton, N.J.: Princeton UP, 1959.

Flying Saucers. Trans. R.F.C. Hull. Bollingen Series XX. Princeton, N.J.; Princeton, UP, 1978.

Kerényi, Karl. *Apollo*. Trans. Jon Solomon. Dallas: Spring, 1983.

Paris, Ginette. *Pagan Meditations*. Trans. Gwendolyn Moore. Woodstock, CT: Spring, 1997.

17) Entertainment:
The Meaning of the Word and Ritual

(Note: This essay was published in the Los Angeles Times on May 1, 2000, with title: "'Entertainment': A Dirty Word?" It was also incorporated into a paper presented at the Midwest Modern Language Association: "Modern Theatre, Entertainment Ritual and the Theories of Cultural Anthropologist Victor Turner" in Kansas City, Missouri, November 2-4, 2000.)

"Entertainment." It's a word we use so often in Los Angeles, home of the "entertainment industry," that we don't think about its meaning anymore. We take it for granted. As a category, entertainment is given a lower-brow status than "the arts," although financially, entertainment is considered the more desirable enterprise. We acknowledge the arts in Los Angeles, but we put food on the table through entertainment.

Popular entertainment deserves more cultural respect than it gets. What would happen if entertainment were recognized for what it does for our souls as well as our pocketbooks? Would that change the way people in the entertainment industry work and the way they "entertain"? The word's archaic meanings indicate that an attitudinal shift toward entertainment is warranted.

Most people are surprised to learn the linguistic heritage of the word "entertainment." We know if something sparks our interest or is amusing or diverting, it is entertaining; we also grasp that to entertain means to offer hospitality or to consider a notion. But its lexical roots show that its original usage was hardly a casual, hospitable or trivial one. Instead, it had a significant function.

From an etymological perspective, the verb derives from two main sources: the French *entretenir*, which means to maintain or hold together, and the Latin *inter* (between) and *tenere* (to hold). These older roots imply that entertainment has a special purpose: to bring an audience to an imaginary "between" world, beyond reality, and to maintain their interest sufficiently to hold them there.

This older meaning also suggests that to entertain is to create a temporary collective; if you can hold a group together, you've centralized and unified a community for a ritual, performance or event—a civic-social-psychological function. Going to a show means you're embarking upon an otherworldly voyage with a bunch of folks, and you won't be leaving your seat. In fact, you'll be held there, riveted, if it's entertaining. Whether a rock concert or an action movie, you are taking part in a communal experience that involves a large, diverse group of people.

Interestingly, the function of "holding together" is shared by "art" and "entertainment," according to the dictionary. Most of us think of the differences between the two categories, but in etymological terms, they share a purpose: containing community. The origin of "arts" is from the Old French *arte* and the Latin *ars* (arts) and *artus* (joint, holding together).

Okay, we all know that you have to hold an audience's attention to entertain them, but to unify a group of people as you take them to an illusive "between" world is a very special calling. U.S. culture in the twenty-first century is more and more fragmented, with new technologies changing our sense of community and interaction. Entertainment is one of the great rituals of American life;

increasingly, studies show that being entertained is perhaps the one national ritual we all share.

Community, unity, sustenance from the imagination: This is what you give an audience when you truly entertain. It is time to recover the full meaning of "entertainment" from those early roots. The ability to hold and unify an audience during a possibly life-changing, aesthetic excursion to the threshold space between the real and the imagined is significant and serious. It fulfills a need of the psyche.

As a category, it deserves more appreciation for the cultural role it plays. More than a revenue-generating industry, it's a national ritual with the ability to unify and heal. *That's* entertainment.

18) Acts of Protest, Athena, and *Lysistrata*

(Note: This essay is published for the first time in this volume.)

"We're going to occupy the Acropolis today."
—Aristophanes' *Lysistrata*[141]

Since the birth and geographic proliferation of the "Occupy Movement," references to Aristophanes' renowned comedy *Lysistrata* as an "archetypal" example of an ancient protest model are more common in popular culture, especially in blogs or newspapers.[142] Aristophanes, a Greek male playwright, was not considered a "feminist" in his time, but *Lysistrata* is certainly about a female collective that works against "the establishment." *Lysistrata*, first presented in Athens in 411 B.C.E., is named for its dedicated protagonist, an ordinary Athenian woman who leads an anti-war revolt based upon a sexual boycott. I began to wonder: How is *Lysistrata* related to modern protests, specifically to contemporary movements involving inequality, seeking societal transformation? Why is it referenced as an "archetypal" protest model in pop culture? Who are the archetypes involved?

Aristophanes is a playwright in the "Old Comedy" tradition.[143] *Lysistrata* is often characterized today as ribald entertainment, but its original purpose cannot be contextualized as merely "lightweight." It is the third and last of Aristophanes' "Peace" plays. Of *Lysistrata*, Alan H. Sommerstein observes: "It is a dream about peace…"[144] At the time of its creation, Athens was engaged in the lengthy, devastating Peloponnesian War. Douglass Parker notes: "*Lysistrata*'s greatness ultimately resides in its sheer nerve, its thoroughgoing audacity in confronting, after twenty years of conflict, an Athens poised between external and internal disasters, between the annihilation of her Sicilian expeditionary force in 413 and the overthrow of her constitution in 411."[145] The original fifth century B.C.E. performance of *Lysistrata* most likely aligned with the Lenaea, a Bacchic winter festival.[146] Sommerstein reminds us that "the very performance of an Aristophanic comedy was itself part of a religious observance."[147] And it is worth noting that a playwright's intentions in writing political satire may be considered thematically as "serious" as those of a tragedian.

I started with a review of the play and a focus on the story.

PLOT

Almost everyone is still asleep, or "unconscious," when the play begins. The implication: it's time to wake people up! In *Lysistrata*, women from Athens, Sparta and beyond are called to a meeting at dawn, organized by a young woman named Lysistrata. She's the first to arrive; she's been kept up many nights with worry about her newly conceived plan. When other women trickle in, Lysistrata reveals her bold scheme: In a move to fight male oppression and to stop the ruination of their war-torn Greece, all women must protest on behalf of their social demands for equality and to bring a peaceful vision to society. Lysistrata entreats them: "The whole future of the country rests with us."[148] And: "I am going to bring it about that no man, for at least a generation, will raise a spear with another."[149] The gathered women wonder: How? Lysistrata explains: First, we must abstain from sex with men. Before Lysistrata commits the women to this collective abstinence protest with a group promise, she reveals their next big move: "We're going to occupy the Acropolis today."[150] The women make a vow of commitment to the cause; as they do, a loud cheer is heard offstage.

Success for "Occupy Treasury at the Acropolis!" The Chorus of Old Women has seized control of the treasury at the Acropolis (near Athena's temple), so that no war expenses may be disbursed. The military assets are, in effect, frozen. Next, the women occupying the Acropolis are confronted with authoritarian force. The Chorus of Old Women must combat the Chorus of Old Men with their fists, and by dousing them—and their fires—with water. Then an officiating magistrate brings a team of fierce Scythian archers (a policing unit) to contain the protesting women. The archers flaunt bows, quivers and whips.[151] The magistrate's slaves carry additional weapons. The magistrate commands: "Let's have the crowbars, and we'll soon put a stop to this nonsense."[152] Before the beatings can begin, Lysistrata and Stratyllis (an older woman) invoke Artemis, Hecate, and the Two Goddesses (Demeter and Persephone) to save them from brutality.

Suddenly, masses of female food workers—now part of the growing activist movement—reveal themselves and swarm the scene. The Archers scatter; the women are saved. Painstakingly, Lysistrata mediates with the remaining magistrate to restore peace; he invokes Zeus, and is not swayed. Lysistrata tells him: "We want to keep the money safe and stop you from waging war."[153] She warns him that the women have control of all the state's funds, adding: "We're going to save you whether you like it or not."[154] Lysistrata declares that the women will be famous throughout their country as great "Liquidators of War."[155]

When others in the protest movement begin to falter, Lysistrata prevails upon the women to stay committed to abstinence—and to their vision of peace. She shows them an oracle that predicts success if they remain unified. They "tease" a husband, who tries to unite with his young wife Myrrhine for a conjugal visit. Myrrhine is lured outside to care for her baby, whom her husband carries to the visit; he tries to appeal to her maternal instincts and begs his wife to end the crusade. However, Myrrhine does not succumb to her husband's pleas for sex and stays with the activists.

Finally, men from various regional factions form a delegation to negotiate an end to the women's protest. A herald arrives with this news. Lysistrata officiates at the peace talks and offers "Reconciliation" in the form of a naked young woman as a symbol of the end of strife.[156] As peace is restored, dancing and festivity ensues; Lysistrata is re-costumed to wear "the aegis of Athena," a sacred honor garment worn by an official priestess of Athena.[157]

MODERN CORRELATIVES

Based on the plot, it is worth noting that there are three elements from *Lysistrata* that parallel aspects of contemporary protest movements:

1) a collective that protests against a form of oppression;
2) the protest action is undertaken to raise awareness, or to provoke/promote change; and
3) the protestors may face a police or an authoritarian presence.

There is a fourth element of *Lysistrata*'s plot that relates specifically to the modern Occupy Movement: wealth and war are "occupied" in both.[158]

Some events from the Occupy Wall Street movement may be linked to these categories above. On September 17, 2011, activists and protestors coalesced into a leaderless protest at Zuccotti Park,[159] in what would famously become the birth of Occupy Wall Street. Their first banner read: "We are the 99 percent."[160] The purpose of this initial activism was to protest gross financial and social inequity as emblematized by the Wall Street financial center in New York. Lynn Parramore of AlterNet.org writes: "A bold idea had sprung from a tiny park: that ordinary people can mount a challenge to the entire economic and political system."[161] This initial intention can be seen as similar to the women in *Lysistrata*'s protest who wish to save the country's future through the Acropolis' (and the treasury's) occupation, and by ending war.

In terms of "occupying war," those in the Occupy Movement joined in anti-war protests during occupations in New York, Washington, D.C., and beyond. The "Declaration of Occupation of New York City" (from the original Occupy Wall Street movement) locates war as the industry of the one percent: "They continue to create weapons of mass destruction in order to receive government contracts."[162] The subsequent document "The 99 percent Declaration," which evolved from the movement, offers a suggested grievance at Number 11 as "Ending Perpetual War For Profit."[163] In other locations around the U.S., members of the Occupy Movement have participated in anti-war demonstrations, such as November 1, 2011, in Occupy L.A. (with a chant of "Stop the wars of the one percent.") and on January 7, 2012, in Occupy Tulsa.

It is worth noting that the physical confrontations between the Occupy Movement and police forces do seem to echo parts of *Lysistrata*. Direct shows of force occur between the two Choruses (of Old Men and Old Women); these episodes end with threats and water-dousing. When the magistrate arrives with an armed policing unit in the middle of the comedy, the protestors are saved by a crowding swarm of other female activists. The demonstrations in the Occupy Movement are planned as creative and non-violent. In their gatherings, too, there are sometimes more protestors than police; this may provide some safety to protestors. The Occupy Movement has faced aggressive policing, such as at Brooklyn Bridge on October 1, 2011, and at the Port of Oakland on November 3, 2011.

ARCHETYPAL ELEMENTS

In *Lysistrata*, gods and goddesses are called upon at various junctures in the satire.[164] Some of the deities directly invoked are: Zeus, Demeter and Persephone (the Two Goddesses), Caster and Pollux (the Two Gods), Persuasion, Aphrodite, Athena, Hecate, Artemis, Eileithyia, Apollo, Poseidon, Hera, Bacchus, Memory (Mnemosyne) and Helen.[165] The use of invocations to so many different deities hints at a pantheon of interested divinities reigning above the earthly action in *Lysistrata*. Could the activism in the play serve a higher cause (or causes), beyond the "mortal" perspective? The males reacting to the protest invoke deities, too. Key characters look to deities for aid and protection throughout. Perhaps the characters even serve, in the moment, in the agency of specific deities.

Aristophanes begins the play with mentions of Pan and Aphrodite, no doubt to set a "sexual" tone; the many bawdy sexual puns in the play have survived through the ages (and varying translations) as well. The plot, involving abstinence from sex, is certainly related to Aphrodite's realm.

In addition to direct invocation, the goddess Athena is also "present" in the play in several ways through: the character of Lysistrata herself; the use of abstinence as political strategy; and the occupation of the Treasury near Athena's temple, which also becomes a stoppage of war and thus a military strategy to achieve peace.[166]

As Judith Fletcher writes in her "Afterword" to the Parker's translation of *Lysistrata*: "To be sure, there is much of Athena in this play." Fletcher points out that key scenes are set on the Acropolis, "where women and girls enacted important rituals in or near Athena's temple, the Parthenon...These considerations lend weight to the speculation that Lysistrata is probably a fictionalized version of a historical woman who actually served as priestess of Athena in the late fifth century B.C.E."[167] In effect, the character of Lysistrata may be seen as Athena's proxy in the play, albeit a mortal agent; this is revealed by playwright Aristophanes directly in a visual image at the end of the show when Lysistrata appears wearing the sacred vestment or "aegis" assigned only to Athena's holy priestesses,[168] indicative of Lysistrata's ascension to a higher stature as an official acolyte—as a reward for her dedicated service to the goddess.

Athens was under Athena's protection; the city-state is named in her honor. Robert E. Bell writes in *Women of Classical Mythology*: "She [Athena] maintained law and order internally and protected the state from external enemies. In times of war she protected fortresses, harbors, and towns. Though she was frequently represented in armor, her warlike attributes were geared more to protectiveness than to aggression...Her principal role was the strengthening of the state within and the civilization of its people."[169] Bell also writes: "Her [Athena's] temples and statues on the Acropolis could be called the center of the political universe."[170] Athena is directly connected to the concept of *polis*, as in "metropolis"; one of her epithets was "Athena Polias."

The women's occupation of the Acropolis' Treasury in the play could be seen as a way for Athena, via her proxy Lysistrata, to re-direct the political/military direction of Athens. She accomplishes this by controlling the distribution of wealth, and thereby ends funding for military operations. Calonice, another female protestor in the play, relates that her husband has been away from home for five months, stationed at the Thracian coast, "keeping an eye on our general there."[171] The end of war may bring family reunification to those in military life, adding another "pro-peace" incentive to the *Lysistrata* protest.

Aristophanes' play *Lysistrata* ends happily, with a peace treaty and a celebration. The female protestors' demands are finally met; their "occupation" is successful. Their leader, Lysistrata, is formerly aligned as an official priestess to the goddess Athena by the end of the play. Did the goddess inspire Lysistrata, as agent-leader, and the female protestors to "right" Athens' course away from war, towards peace, and a more "civilized" life in the *polis*? It is a possible interpretation.

RELEVANCE TO CONTEMPORARY TIMES

The plot parallels from *Lysistrata* to contemporary protests are noted in a previous section. But do archetypal aspects of *Lysistrata* also connect to modern activism today in terms of the psyche? Is this why the play's title shows up frequently in electronic and print media, most recently in reference to the Occupy Movement? Modern protest movements could certainly be seen as serving a "higher cause"; they involve an entire community or a large group of like-minded individuals with shared goals. The various deities invoked in *Lysistrata* may also relate to the contemporary notion of an advisory council who guides a modern protest movement (such as a board), or to activist figures of inspiration who mentor those who challenge the status quo in order to bring about societal change. This concept could be linked to the function of elders or former leaders who advise modern protest movements.

The goddess Athena, with her association to the concept of *polis* and her links to strategy and planning, may have psychic resonance related to community transformation through protest. Modern social protests require strategies involving teams, groups, avenues, energies, supplies, funds—not unlike the planning needed in ancient military operations. And a protest is a fight against something, by definition; in a protest, there is a metaphoric tie to battle, at the very least. Lysistrata, as protagonist, is the one who raises the initial protest to consciousness, organizes and bonds their group together, sends out teams in strategic waves, ensures the protest group coheres, and in the end negotiates the peace.

Through her acolyte-proxy Lysistrata, Athena mediates between oppositional factions with success and a new era begins as a result of the "occupation." Near the end of the play, Lysistrata says: "let us have a dance of Thanksgiving—/And let us for the future all endeavor/Not to repeat our errors never ever."[172] Thus, Lysistrata ends the protest, and joins the various factions together with a group dance, an inclusive symbolic ceremonial ritual.

Returning to my own understanding of protests and activism in contemporary times, and to my inquiry as to why *Lysistrata* is referenced in pop culture or media as a protest prototype: I believe that Aristophanes' *Lysistrata* does provide a basic activism template, with key points that still resonate with the contemporary psyche. A collective non-violent protest against oppression by taking on the establishment; working to raise awareness and bring about change; facing a policing unit: all are part of recent events in modern activism. The "occupation of wealth and war" in *Lysistrata* especially resonates with the missions of the Occupy Movement.

Aristophanes' satire reminds us, too, that "the divine" may be a part of a protest movement, either through direct agency such as through an acolyte or a deity "proxy," or metonymically through an invocation, or simply above "in spirit." It reminds us of the goddess Athena's connection to the foundations of modern civilization. It presents the idea that a civil protest may occur under Athena's aegis, perhaps as a way to balance and adjust the status of the *polis*. Athena is, after all, the "savior of cities."[173]

[141] Aristophanes' *Lysistrata and Other Plays*, Trans. Alan H. Sommerstein. London: Penguin Classics, 2002. Line 176, p. 147.
[142] For two representative headline examples, please see:
1) The *Ms. Blog* entry by Holly L. Derr for November 29, 2011, mentions a production of the play in an activist event round-up, next to an "Occupy" reference:
http://msmagazine.com/blog/blog/2011/11/29/dont-ms-lysistrata-radical-women-occupying-relationships-between-white-and-black-women-and-more/.
2) *The Modesto Bee*, November 24, 2011, references "Occupy" in relationship to a local production of *Lysistrata*.
http://www.modbee.com/2011/11/23/1960275/mjc-occupies-akropolis-with-its.html.
Also related is the Lysistrata Project [lysistrata.org] which was founded in 2002, in order to promote peace after 9-11.
[143] Aristophanes' *Lysistrata and Other Plays*, Trans. Alan H. Sommerstein. London: Penguin Classics, 2002. Sommerstein, "Introduction," p. xix. For more on "Old Comedy," please see:
http://en.wikipedia.org/wiki/Ancient_Greek_comedy.
[144] *Ibid.*, Sommerstein, "Preface to Lysistrata," p. 133.
[145] "Introduction" by Douglass Parker. *Aristophanes' Lysistrata: A Modern Translation* by Douglass Parker. New York: Penguin, 2009, p. 12.
[146] "Afterword" by Judith Fletcher, *Aristophanes' Lysistrata: A Modern Translation* by Douglass Parker. New York: Penguin, 2009, p. 138.
[147] "Introduction." Aristophanes' *Lysistrata and Other Plays*, Trans. Alan H. Sommerstein. London: Penguin Classics, 2002., p. xxiii.
[148] Sommerstein, line 33, p. 142.
[149] *Ibid.*, lines 49-50, p. 142.
[150] See Note 141 for citation. As a comparison, Parker's translation reads: "We're taking over the Acropolis…" p. 36.
[151] Sommerstein, p. 156. The list of weaponry varies per translation, per edition.
[152] Sommerstein, line 425, p. 157.
[153] *Ibid.*, line 488, p. 159.
[154] *Ibid.*, line 498, p. 160.
[155] *Ibid.*, line 554, p. 162.
[156] In the Douglass translation, she is named "Peace," a handmaid to Lysistrata, p. 115.
[157] Sommerstein, 191/Note 163, p. 240.
[158] Some note that there is a gender parity movement within the Occupy Movement as well; please see Susan Smith, for one examination of this:

"Occupying Women's Issues: Gender and the Occupy Movement." December 6, 2011.
http://www.hercampus.com/school/upenn/occupying-womens-issues-gender-and-occupy-movement.
[159] Later, the space's original title was restored: Liberty Plaza.
[160] Lynn Parramore, "Introduction." *99%: How the Occupy Wall Street Movement is Changing America*. Don Hazen, Tara Lohan and Lynn Parramore, eds. San Francisco: AlterNet Books, 2011, p. 12.
[161] *Ibid.*, p. 13.
[162] "Declaration of the Occupation of New York City" written by the New York City General Assembly, accepted by the New York General Assembly on September 29, 2011:
http://www.commondreams.org/view/2011/10/02-1.This formal document could also be seen as relatable to the oath of loyalty taken by the female protest collective in *Lysistrata*.
[163] "The 99% Declaration," by The 99% Working Group, https://sites.google.com/site/the99percentdeclaration/.
[164] The invocations vary per translation, per edition.
[165] Helen was worshipped as a deity in Sparta, as mother and wife. For more on "Helen the pure," see Sommerstein, Note 170, pps. 240-1. Among the other gods and goddesses mentioned/inferred, though not directly invoked, are: Pan, Adonis, Medusa, Cybele, Eros, The Amazons, Hestia, Atalanta (via a mention of Melanion), Heracles, and The Furies. Again, these mentions/inferences vary per translation, per edition.
[166] For more about the goddess Athena, please see "Pieces of Athena (and Her Head)" in this volume.
[167] Judith Fletcher, "Afterward." *Aristophanes' Lysistrata: A Modern Translation* by Douglass Parker. New York: Penguin, 2009, pps. 143-144.
[168] See Sommerstein, p. 191.
[169] Robert E. Bell, *Women of Classical Mythology*. Oxford: Oxford UP, 1991, p. 85.
[170] *Ibid.*, p. 86.
[171] Sommerstein, p. 145.
[172] Sommerstein, line 1276, p. 191.
[173] From Homeric "Hymn 28 to Athena," Hugh G. Evelyn-White (trans.) Tufts University. Perseus Hopper. 2 Feb. 2012.
http://www.perseus.tufts.edu/hopper/text;jsessionid=77F0F2DDC280C25D3E6AB4F2E61FCB1C?doc=Perseus%3atext%3a1999.01.0137%3ahymn%3d28.

19) Matters of the Heart and Soul: Courtly Love

(Note: This essay is published for the first time in this volume. Courtly love is always a popular motif in literature, the arts, and film, sometimes when we least expect it. "Drive" [2011] with Ryan Gosling and Carey Mulligan, for instance, is a postmodern example of the courtly love motif in film.)

The twelfth century courtly love (or *cortezia/amour courtois*) movement has fascinated scholars for centuries. At the beginning of the twenty-first century, the movement furthered by the troubadours is still popular. In the twentieth century, many respected academicians published books addressing the topic, including C. S. Lewis, Denis de Rougement, L.T. Topsfield, and Joseph Campbell. There are powerful romantic echoes in popular culture as well; hit movies, best-selling books, and Broadways musicals fictionally depict aspects of the courtly love movement.[174] Why so much interest? What is the relevancy of this arcane, provincial albeit "comprehensive cultural phenomenon"[175] to our modern, broadbanded global village?

There is a spiritual resonance to the courtly love movement that is timeless; it highlights principles of love, honor, altruism, personal happiness, death, and finally, a dedication to the Highest Good. These tenets, espoused by the troubadours, directly affect the tending of the soul. To that end, the *cortezia/amour courtois* (including our postmodern "revisionist" reflections on it) is an important key to rediscovering transcendental values of the human spirit.

In order to examine the spiritual aspects of this movement in details, it is necessary to briefly trace its basic definitions, its origins, its developmental stages, and the etymology of the word "troubadour." The mores of the phenomenon merit study, as well as the lexicon of the troubadours. Finally, the specific works of two troubadours who wrote directly about matters of the heart and soul, Guilhem IX of Aquitane and Guiraut Riquier, warrant analysis for their major contributions to this movement.

Courtly love is, according to C.S. Lewis in his book *The Allegory of Love*: "love of a highly specialized sort, whose characteristics may be enumerated as Humility, Courtesy, Adultery, and the Religion of Love. The lover is always abject. Obedience to his lady's lightest wish…and silent acquiescence…are the only virtues he dares to claim."[176] By putting a lady's needs ahead of his own, a knight/poet becomes "courteous." According to Lewis, "only the courteous can love, but it is love that makes them courteous."[177] Lewis points out that this love is modeled on the paradigm of feudal service and usually directed at a "lady" who is another man's wife. Thus, the intrinsic points of the lovers may participate in the "play" or mimetic desire of the phenomenon.[178] Some sociologists suggest that it was due, in part, to the shortage of women in the aristocracy in the south of France that "another man's wife" would be so desirable.[179]

A knight's devoted service to another man's wife can only produce tension if it goes "unsatisfied"—which it must, in order to conform to the standards of courtly love. This paradox of unconsummated, passionate ardor versus devoted, altruistic service is fundamental to this movement. Denis de Rougemont, in his famous work *Passion and Society* writes: "What a strange love (it will be thought) that thus conforms to laws whereby it stands condemned in order the better to preserve itself!"[180] De Rougemont offers an explanation of its development: "The cultivation of passionate love began in Europe as a reaction to Christianity (and in particular to the doctrine of marriage) by people whose spirit, whether naturally or by inheritance was still pagan."[181] Therefore, the movement evolved in direct response to spiritual conflict: the end of "pagan" values colliding with Christian doctrines.

Scholar Roger Boase, in his study *The Origin and Meaning of Courtly Love*, defined the phenomenon and its genesis as: "a literary movement, an ideology, an ethical system, a style of life, and an expression of play element in culture, which arose in an aristocratic Christian environment exposed to Hispano-Arabic influence. This phenomenon occurred in the south of France..."[182] Boase elaborates on its roots by tracing them to the "paradoxical expression" of Sufi poetry, specifically Ibn al Arabi.[183] Boase attributes "the conventional dichotomies of troubadour poetry, in particular the love-death equation" to Sufi literature.[184] It was thought honorable, even desirable, to die for one's love; it was the penultimate expression of passion. Profiling its genesis further, Boase credits "the cosmology of Empedocles and Heraclitus" as an additional influence "in the development of a paradoxical courtly style, justified by a theory of universal strife."[185] Heraclitus' concept of holding something and its opposite, the "both/and," is evident in the philosophy of courtly love. The tension is there between both verbalizing passionate, carnal feelings and not satisfying them, e.g. maintaining chastity. This dynamic is also often present in devoted altruism: by serving the married "lady" and her needs, the knight/poet may ultimately further the estate as a whole, the greater good, when the wife's goals mesh with those of her husband's goals. Thus, the lover may end up serving both the lady and the opposite—his rival, a feudal lord.

This system began to be immortalized in troubadourian poetry, and thus popularized, at the end of the eleventh century, "when Guilhem IX Duke of Aquitane began to compose."[186] It lasted until 1323, roughly two hundred fifty years.[187] There are four main developmental stages of the movement, as defined by scholar J. T. Topsfield in his book *Troubadours and Love.* There is early poetry written near the beginning of the twelfth century, which is not about courtly ideas of behavior but focuses on the individual's quest for happiness. The second period is delineated by the influence at Poitiers of Eleanor of Aquitane, and lasts from about 1150 to 1180. Poetry from this time is marked by a conflict between the soulful, reflective creations of the troubadour and the courts' demands for a lighter style. In the third section, from 1180 to 1209, the "light," courtly style of poetry replaced the former; it is during this golden era of the troubadours that many famous works emanated from the minor courts of Languedoc, Provence, and Augerene.[188]

In 1209, there is a major shift which brings about the end of troubadourian poetry—thus, the final stage: "At the moment of greatest poetic richness and social splendour, the axe of the Albigensian Crusade falls on the noble society of the South. Courtly society in many areas is decimated, and in the changed world of the late thirteenth century love for the courtly lady or *domna* is transformed into love for the Virgin."[189] It is interesting to note the shift from love of "Ladies" to Marianism as the final thrust of troubadourian poetry; the spiritual implications in this stage are evident; the concept of love was so "pure" (*amor pur*) and heightened that the next evolution in its development was symbolic: worship.

Even the etymology of the word "troubadour" belies its creative and spiritual resonance. Its origin has been a subject of heated debate among scholars. Boase limits the etymological discussion in his book to two pages in the appendix, but finds its roots to be a combining of *trobar* and *amor heroes*.[190]

Trobar is thought to be related to the Provençal verb *trobar* and the old French verb *trouver*. Both verbs denote composing, inventing, or finding "new melodies."[191] However, the roots are also known to have Arabic influence; the Arabic word *tarab* means 'music or song' and the verb *daraba* means 'to strike,' as in the playing of a stringed instrument.[192] Certainly the creating of something new—and the cathartic act of performing it in public—suggests a healing purpose to this ritual. The act of troubadourian performance may even be classified as a ceremonial healing experience; it certainly qualifies as "a re-enactment of the great myths" that may be "effective through the sheer beauty of the rites, the costumes, the music, and the dances."[193]

Amor heroes is a cerebral love malady brought upon by Eros. A combination of Greek (*eros*), Arabic (*al-ishq*) and Latin (*herus*), the term came into use through the work of physicians, who were trying to diagnose maladies. The term was eventually used by Chaucer in "The Knight's Tale."[194] It was often fatal: those afflicted with it "would slowly fade away and die unless they were united with the object of their love (which was often kept secret)."[195] Boase surmises that the term "denoted a species of melancholia to which lovers were prone" and "elucidates certain aspects of Courtly Love, in particular, the belief in the potentially destructive power of Love."[196] He further identifies nobility as being especially susceptible to this malady and concludes: "These destructive and paradoxical effects of love were...an integral part of the Courtly Love tradition."[197]

The distinct mores of the courtly love tradition were officially (and contemporaneously) codified by Andreas Capellanus (also known as Andreas the Chaplain) in his books *De Amore* and *De Arte Honeste Amandi*. Spenserian specialist Earle Fowler detailed the Capellanus code in his book *Spenser and the System of Courtly Love*: "According to these laws, the *villain* [sic] is excluded from love-making. Absolute loyalty, obedience, vassalage, and secrecy are required of the lover. He must be willing to suffer dishonor for his lady. He must believe no evil of her and defend her honor."[198] Additional requirements were neatness in appearance and a joyful attitude. It was also vital that "the pleasure of the beloved"[199] not be exceeded.[200]

Joseph Campbell, in *Creative Mythology*, characterized the "cult of *amor*" as insanity-inducing: "And finally, the mad disciplines to which a lover might, in the name of love, subject himself, sometimes approached the lunacies of a penitential grove."[201] Campbell observes that "nature in its noblest moment—the realization of love—is an end and glory in itself; and the sense, ennobled and refined by courtesy and art, temperance, loyalty and courage, as the guides to this realization."[202] A further distinction is made by Campbell in regards to the customs of these rites; it is a personal journey as opposed to a communal one. It requires individuation and discrimination on the part of the lovers, as they embark through this daring gateway to seek the heart's satisfaction.[203] Ecstasy was a desired end to this journey as the lovers seek to merge, engage in an amatory trance, or become lost in the mere contemplation of each other's image.[204]

In *The System of Courtly Love*, Lewis F. Mott writes: "The butterflies die, and the loves of the troubadours were, not infrequently, ended by the sudden hand of death. The heartfelt laments which burst forth from the depths of earnest grief soon became a conventional habit of mourning."[205] Thus, mourning, eulogy, and a constant awareness of "the tyranny of Death" made the lovers' causes all the more desperate and bittersweet, fueling the flames of passion.[206] The reverse was also highly possible: a knight/poet might die in battle or in service to his Lady. The component of death made the participants all the more aware of the preciousness of life; a heightened idealization of love was thus enforced by the ever-impending sword. There is an implied martyrdom here that certainly has religious resonance.

The rise of Marianism through troubadourian poetry indicates, even more directly, an "immediate" search for God and spiritual redemption. The mysticism inherent in the cult of the Virgin Mary was a favored topic of the poets after 1230. Some of these tributes were banned. As Boase notes, the troubadours "were under increasing pressure, when the Albigensian Crusade ended in 1229, to make their poetry conform to ecclesiastical requirements."[207] But the worship of Mary could not be subdued, and finally, the church authorities deemed it "preferable to outright heresy."[208] The smooth transition from a pure love to religious worship is even further evidence of the nature of the rituals of Courtly Love; if Courtly Love were merely carnal in purpose, for example, the deification of the Virgin Mary through troubadourian verse (and public acceptance of it) would not have so readily occurred.

The lexicon used by the troubadours and courtiers specifically reflects matters of the soul. The courtly terminology and various classifications of troubadourian poetry clearly indicates that the purposes of the songs were profoundly ambitious, and beyond mere "entertainment." In just a few examples, these higher goals are readily apparent. A *courtesia* is a summation of all courtly virtues and the related social behaviors. A *devinalh* is a riddle poem which usually needed some sort of hint or "key" to its solution, a mystery. This type of song often had religious/mystic connotations. A *jovens* is a term indicating a celebration of youth and generosity of spirit. A *mesura* was the rational balance between the demands of the court and the "talents, aspirations, and quality of the individual" or moderation.[209] A *sirventes* was a poem with a moral point. *Valors* indicated "innate moral worth."[210] So much in troubadourian verse is related to goodness—and the ability to impart this goodness to the court-at-large. Religion, celebrations of spirit and moral worth are subjects that lead to the examination of matters of the soul. It also, by nature, brought out the best in a suitor, setting a standard for moral excellence, according to Maurice Keen: "Troubadour lyric, which was essentially introspective, sought to express the overwhelming force of adulatory passion, inspired by a beloved woman, which force it interpreted as the source of all excellence and endeavor in him whom it bound to her service."[211]

A brief look at a few lines of writing from two famous troubadours—one from the beginning of the era and another from the end—clearly reveals the transcendent nature of the work.

Guilhem IX of Aquitane, who lived from 1071 to 1127, was a successful warrior as well as the first "troubadourian" poet.[212] He wrote of the standards of excellence in the court (and reciprocity) in his poem "Ben vuelh": "If men of excellence find pleasure in my company, I am quite aware that I must in return desire their trust and their entertainment."[213] The same poem also extols the necessity of the "ability to distinguish wisdom from folly, shame from honour, the need for boldness or timidity and the better side to choose in a debate on love."[214] These are subjects of "right/good" versus "wrong/evil," but moreover, they are topics which assert a higher realm. Guilhem IX of Aquitane challenges all members of the court to live by a higher code. This level of discernment extended beyond the observation of courtly mores. Indeed, Guilhem IX was able to distinguish "the planes of love" with equal facility. He divides love into three categories in his songs: physical desire within the court, "dream-like imagining" of the love object or "illusory joy," and "a 'transcendental' plane which offers him a supreme joy from which good results flow."[215] The third category is most directly related to a spiritual love.

Near the end of the troubadourian era, Giraut Riquier, who composed from 1270 through 1285, also distinguished the trifurcated nature of love in his poetic commentary "Epistle VIII." He delineated: "heavenly love, natural love of kinsfolk, and carnal love which is the lowest form of love."[216] Of carnal love, Riquier comments: "It is unbridled, devoid of clear judgment, listening only to desire and not to reason...This love disappears once it has been fulfilled." Riquier praises the love of God as the highest form of love. He says it is "peace without end, love without restriction, perfect bliss without harm, pleasure without sadness, and joy without desire."[217] Riquier offers a balm for the soul here; "Epistle VIII" won an award in a competition in the court of Rodez in 1280, earning Riquier a diploma.[218] Since his comments garnered a prize, these were standards embraced by the court-at-large. Riquier also declares that troubadours are "favoured by God and the mark of this favour is the wisdom and knowledge [*saber*] which they display in their divine mission as poets."[219] Riquier says that a troubadour is on a mission and that mission is spiritual enlightenment.

The end of the troubadourian movement came about with the decay of "courtly love" in France. The Inquisition, war, economic and social change eliminated its function. Through troubadourian reflections on love, honor, altruism, personal happiness, death, and God, their work set high standards for the social mores and spiritual values of their times. Cathartic healing was evident in the performance aspects of their songs. Through examination of the troubadourian/courtly love movement, we become more in tune with aspects of human existence often lost or ignored in the modern world. The vestiges of the movement remain, forever to be recycled in the films, literature, and theatre of popular culture, due to its therapeutic appeal and spiritual resonance.

---

[174] To name just a few, these include: movies like *Camelot* [1967, & a 2011 TV series], *Excalibur [1981]*, *The Princess Bride* {1987], *First Knight* [1995] or *A Knight's Tale* [2001], and even postmodern takes on courtly love such as *Drive* [2011]; novels like *The Once and Future King* by T.H. White, *The Mists*

of Avalon by Marion Zimmer Bradley, and *The Return of Merlin* by Deepak Chopra; and popular musicals like *Camelot* and *Man of La Mancha*.

[175] Roger Boase, *The Origin and Meaning of Courtly Love*. Manchester, Eng., Manchester University Press, 1977, p. 129.

[176] C.S. Lewis, *The Allegory of Love*. London: Oxford University Press, 1936, p. 2.

[177] *Ibid.*, p. 2.

[178] *Ibid.*, pps. 2-3.

[179] Boase, p. 90.

[180] Denis de Rougemont, *Passion and Society*. Trans. Montgomery Belgion. London: Faber and Faber Ltd., 1956, p. 35.

[181] de Rougemont, p. 74.

[182] Boase, pps. 129-30.

[183] *Ibid.*, p. 124.

[184] *Ibid.*, p. 125.

[185] Boase, p. 124.

[186] L.T. Topsfield, *Troubadors and Love*. Cambridge: Cambridge University Press, 1975, p. 2.

[187] *Ibid.*, p. 2.

[188] *Ibid.*, p. 2.

[189] *Ibid.*, pps. 2-3.

[190] Boase, p. 131.

[191] *Ibid.*, p. 131.

[192] *Ibid.*, p. 131.

[193] Henri Ellenberger, *The Discovery of the Unconscious*. New York: Basic Books, 1979, pps. 28-9.

[194] Boase, p. 132.

[195] Ellenberger, p. 25.

[196] Boase, p. 131.

[197] *Ibid.*, p. 133.

[198] Earle B. Fowler, *Spenser and the System of Courtly Love*. New York: Pharton Press, 1968, p. 2.

[199] Fowler, p. 2.

[200] Chrétien de Troyes is also known to have codified the rituals of courtly love unofficially in his fiction.

[201] Joseph Campbell, *The Masks of the Gods: Creative Mythology, Volume Four*. New York: Penguin, 1968, p. 175.

[202] *Ibid.*, p. 176.

[203] *Ibid.*, pps. 176-7.

[204] Boase, p. 84.

[205] Lewis Freeman Mott, *The System of Courtly Love*, New York: Haskell House, 1965, p. 109.
[206] *Ibid.*, p. 109.
[207] Boase, p. 85.
[208] *Ibid.*, p. 127.
[209] Topsfield, p. 256.
[210] *Ibid.*, p. 257.
[211] Maurice Keen, *Chivalry*. New Haven: Yale University Press, 1984, p. 30.
[212] Topsfield, p. 11.
[213] Qtd. in Topsfield, p. 15.
[214] *Ibid.*, p. 15.
[215] *Ibid.*, p. 26.
[216] Qtd. in Topsfield, p. 251.
[217] *Ibid.*, p. 251.
[218] *Ibid.*, pps. 250-1.
[219] *Ibid.*, p. 250.

20) Facing the Dragon: Of Presidential Nominees and Acceptance Speeches

(This essay is published for the first time in this volume. 2012 is a presidential election year in the U.S. Every time an incumbent politician faces a challenger, aspects of the Combat Myth may be present. The nomination acceptance speech of a presidential candidate is certainly one of the biggest events to watch for signs of the forthcoming rhetorical "battles" in the U.S. presidential campaign season.)

When an American presidential candidate accepts his or her party's presidential nomination at a national convention, it is a defining moment, a spectacular high point of political ritual in the United States.

Traditionally, the nominee's personality, values, and goals are voiced in a nationally televised speech delivered to cheering supporters; this is the culminating nomination acceptance speech, and its ending is punctuated with pageantry: the presentation of the nominee's entire family onstage; and celebration symbols, such as confetti, loud music, and red, white, and blue balloons falling from the rafters. This same speech serves as a foundation for the nominee's appearances and statements along the campaign trail. The nomination acceptance speech is a cornerstone of a candidate's campaign—an outline, a preview, or a promise of what his/her presidency will entail. It presents a complete political platform in microcosm; its rhetorical modalities are representative of the candidate's societal agenda. A nominee's rhetorical template must showcase the public servant's potency as an agent of social change. Julia Kristeva observes in *Language the Unknown: An Initiation into Linguistics*: "...It is an objective law that every social transformation is accompanied by a rhetorical transformation, that every social transformation is in a certain and very profound sense a rhetorical change."[220]

The acceptance speech references the politician's strengths, accomplishments, dreams, and alludes to both allies and enemies; in mythic terms, it is "the hero's or heroine's narrative," and establishes "the team." It is also a chance to heal political rifts within parties, and to establish firmly the nominee as a public leader of the group. James E. Campbell writes in *The American Campaign*: "Most speeches from the faction winning the nomination are conciliatory in tone and stress the common values within the party and the stark differences with the opposition party."[221] According to Campbell, conventions and the nomination acceptance speeches typically mark the end of the nomination process and the beginning of the most vigorous portion of the campaign[222]—thus the speech serves a ritual purpose as a seminal turning point of closure in terms of nominee selection and the beginning of the full campaign on behalf of the party's ticket. The language patterns and properties of the nomination acceptance speech, as well as key points in content, are repeated and expanded upon in public discourse throughout ensuing months, becoming a significant component of the modern candidate's "brand" in the campaign.[223]

In this essay, one nomination acceptance speech, as representative of a modern "standard" presidential nomination acceptance speech in American politics, will be examined. From August 2000, the 53-minute speech presented by candidate George

W. Bush, in Philadelphia, Pennsylvania, at the Republican convention will be analyzed.[224] Combining observations from the use of two different lenses, that of literary criticism and mythological studies, new characteristics may be unpacked.

Most, if not all, presidential candidates use professional speechwriters, especially during national campaigns, and nominee Governor George W. Bush in 2000 was no exception. However, for the purposes of this essay, it is the final speech transcript, with *ad libs* and spontaneous changes from the candidate "in performance" that will be analyzed instead of the "official" version released in advance, which contains only the prepared text. Therefore, authorship, for these analytical purposes, is attributed to the candidate himself and not his speechwriting team.

COMBAT MYTH AND CAMPAIGN RHETORIC

Although "campaign" was originally a military term, its use to describe political competition is American. "Campaign" evolved from several language sources: from the French word *campagne*, derived from the Italian *campagna*, which means "field or military operation"; and from Late Latin *campnia*, which denotes "open country, battlefield," and which comes from Latin *campus* or "field." The etymological roots of "campaign" belie its military origins. By the late eighteenth century, however, the word began to designate an "action to obtain an end." By 1809, it was applied to "activities to get someone elected." The country where this usage shift first occurred was the United States of America, according to Michael Quinion, the creator and author of the website WorldWideWords.org.[225]

Joseph Fontenrose, in *Python, A Study of Delphic Myth and Its Origin*, defines a combat myth as a story in which "a god fights a dragon,"[226] related to the epic battle between an old and new order; Fontenrose states that the plot of the combat myth has "descended from a common original, an archetype."[227] The two central combat myths in Fontenrose's study are Apollo's battle with the chthonic earth-dragon Python and the Zeus-Typhon myth. In *A Dictionary of Symbols*, Jean Chevalier and Alain Gheerbrant note: "Apollo's victory over the serpent is that of reason over instinct, of consciousness over the unconscious."[228] In his Conclusion, Fontenrose says: "The combat-myth is a myth of beginnings, a tale of conflict between order and disorder, chaos and cosmos."[229] Kenneth Burke, in "Myth, Poetry and Philosophy," writes positively of the breadth of Fontenrose's book, beyond its folkloristic approach: "it impinges upon problems of poetics."[230] Burke notes that Fontenrose profiles two main types of the combat myth in his research: "a struggle between an 'older' god and a 'new' god, with the new one triumphing and founding a cult; but this is said to be derived from an earlier type concerning a struggle between dragon and sky god," with the sky god emerging victorious.[231] Apollo took over Python's home after slaying the dragon, and the oracle with it. At the oracle of Delphi, the priestess was called Pythia, a nod to its origin.

Fontenrose's key combat myth plot points include:

1) An extraordinary, avaricious Enemy of divine origin who appears on the scene.

2) This Enemy plots against celestial forces and a divine Champion must confront him.

3) The Champion nearly loses this cosmic fight, but through superior wit, deception or magical charm, eventually vanquishes the Enemy.

4) The Champion celebrates by purifying any "blood pollution" and then institutes "cult, ritual, festival" and founds a new temple in his own name.[232] Another name

for the combat myth, according to Burke, is "The Victory Myth."[233]

Burke applies Fontenrose's combat myth precepts to poetics, rhetoric, and mentions its "specific 'propagandistic' utility."[234] Of the importance of establishing a cult, Burke notes: "A cult is a system of governance."[235] Burke also attaches cyclical succession and seasonal change as reasons for the combat myth's function.[236] The "perfect" combat is between two divinities, Burke writes, as they have equal status; Fontenrose sees the purpose of the combat myth as *aition*, or as Burke describes it: "a story to account for the cult or the services associated with it."[237]

From Burke's observations of Fontenrose's work, it is possible to apply aspects of the combat myth to the presidential nominating process of the modern American election. The fight between "divine" champions in order to establish or to serve a cult could be seen as relatable to nominees who represent their political parties in a fight to "ascend" to the presidency or retain control of it. The concept of "divine" opponents, one representing the "old order," is also relatable to the combat myth.

Sample headlines from media sources in Campaign 2000 read: "Rivals Down to the Heavy Artillery" and "Justices Take Up Florida Battle." Daily cable television shows were titled "Battle for the White House" and "Struggle for the White House." Vice President Albert Gore, Bush's 2000 opponent, used as a recurring campaign mantra: "I will fight for you." Throughout the fall of 2000, the Texas Governor's website published this header: "Help George W. Bush and his fight on the road to the White House…" Artillery, battle, struggle, fights: national campaign rhetoric from both major candidates in 2000 used combat analogies.

To begin the analysis, I will examine George W. Bush's 2000 G.O.P. Nomination Acceptance Speech through the lens of literary criticism.

LITERARY DEVICES

I) Refrains

"A refrain is a phrase, line, or stanza that is repeated periodically in a poem" (Minot 414). Bush's speech borrows from poetic sound devices in its employment of repetitive phrases and lines that may be classified as refrains. The refrain-response oration technique is a common feature in religious litanies, sermons, or rituals and part of many American worship services.

> 1) "This administration had their moment. They've had their chance. They have not led. We will." Parts of these four sentences were echoed in three variant phrases that repeat enough of the original word grouping to resonate as refrains:
>
>> A) "This administration had its chance. They have not led. We will."
>> B) "They had their moment. They have not led. We will."
>> C) "They had their chance. They have not led. We will."
>
> 2) The second refrain that was used was: "On principle." Its first mention was in the sentence: "And I will act on principle." The topic was tax relief. "On principle" was repeated twice more.
>
> 3) "...It won't be long now." This was the most used refrain in the speech, appearing in the peroration. "The wait has been long but it won't be long now." Variants are repeated four more times, for a total of five, but the

variants are introduced with the conjunction "and" instead of "but."

Thus, the refrains used three times or more in the entire speech are: "…They have not led. We will…On principle…And it won't be long now." Refrains appear at the close of the first third of the speech, right before the halfway point, and in the ending.

Two other phrases were repeated twice in *ad libs*; although not planned refrains, these fit into this category, as they were heard by the public and said by the candidate. "Thank you for this honor" was repeated twice in a row in the opening 30 seconds of this speech. "That's a fact" was repeated twice near the halfway point of the speech.

II) Jokes

Depending on the nature of the situation, a politician tells a joke to "break the ice" in a formal speech; it is seen as a way to reveal the politician's humanity and "relatable" personality. The jokes politicians choose to share are important; according to Paul Kugler in *The Alchemy of Discourse*, who attributes the point to Jung, jokes point to unconscious images. Kugler writes: "For Jung, however, the language of the unconscious was not a more primitive and infantile expression, but the voice of nature itself. It is a voice naturally speaking in pun, slips of the tongue, plays on words, and jokes."[238]

Bush told seven jokes in his acceptance speech: two in his introduction, five ridiculing Gore and the Democrats.

His first joke highlighted his own middle initial, to distinguish his candidacy from his father's presidency, former President George Walker Herbert Bush, Sr., and to link his candidacy to another president, the first president of the United States: "Ben Franklin was here. Thomas Jefferson was here. And, of course, George Washington—or, as his friends called him, 'George W.'"

Thus, his first joke identified Bush with the image of the Father: the founding fathers and his own father.

His second joke was about his mother. "Growing up, she gave me love and lots of advice. I gave her white hair." The first joke referencing "father" imagery did not mention physical attributes, but built on patrician values, in a general sense. This second joke specifically referenced a specific physical attribute of Barbara Bush; the joke also implies that as a son, Bush was a source of concern for his mother.

Near the midway point of the speech, the second set of jokes lampoons Gore and the Democrats. Comedians use a technique known as "the callback" which is similar to a refrain; through repetition, a joke may link several subjects together with a repeated line. Using the "callback" technique, the comedian repeats a line frequently, interspersed with description that is qualified by the callback. In this speech, "risky scheme" is the callback. "Our nation today needs a vision. That's a fact. That's a fact. Or, as my opponent might call it, 'a risky truth scheme.'" In using this callback, Bush lampoons Gore's attitudes on the moonwalk, the invention of electricity, and the creation of the Internet (a reference to a statement made by Gore in 1999 and later amended, in which Gore took credit for the invention and promotion of major computer technology). In generating laughter about his opponent, Bush attempts to deflate Gore's *gravitas* and to depict Gore as overly fearful: "But the only thing he [Gore] has to offer is fear itself."

III) One Unfinished Anecdote

A story is a narrative, a recounting of a past event or an imaginary one. Usually, a story has characters and a plot. Bush does complete anecdotes in his speech, but he tells part of one story in his speech without a conclusion.

In the final third of the speech, several short paragraphs are devoted to a description of a Bush visit to a juvenile jail in Marlin,

Texas. Bush recounts dialogue from one of the young offenders. A young man asks then-Governor Bush: "'What do you think of me?'" Bush uses this story as a platform to discuss other "disenfranchised" members of American society: struggling, single mothers; immigrants; fatherless children in gangs, including drug users. Bush seemingly identifies all these groups as "Other" by saying the boy is really asking if a "white man in a suit" cares about "a small voice, but it speaks for so many."

However, Bush never reveals how he answered the young man's question. The story, or plot, is left hanging, unresolved. Although Bush finished his train of thought with ideological points about the dangers of big government, there is an unresolved image present related to the "Other" and the hero. There is an incomplete aspect of the hero's story, beyond the acknowledgment of a problem, a need.

IV) Liturgy, Use of Metonymy

Two parts of Bush's speech replicate language of Christian religious doctrine: *The Lord's Prayer* and *The Apostle's Creed*.

The fragment of *The Lord's Prayer* occurs at the beginning of the speech, as Bush speaks of his father's generation: "A generation of Americans who stormed beaches, liberated concentration camps and delivered us from evil." The line "Lead us not into temptation and deliver us from evil" is the phrase from *The Lord's Prayer* that is referenced, through metonymy. A patriarchal symmetry can be seen in relating the father to "Our Father" (*Pater Noster*): "And so, when I put my hand on *The Bible*, I will swear to not only uphold the laws of our land, I will swear to uphold the honor and dignity of the office to which I have been elected, so help me God."[239] Bush presents the image of placing his hand on *The Bible* at a presidential inauguration ceremony, thus correlating the image of America's "father" in service of the Father.

Next, he introduces a long section in which he states his beliefs. An edited version below shows the pattern "I believe" at the beginning of seven lines in this section [italics mine]: "*I believe* the presidency—the final point of decision in the American government—was made for great purposes...*I believe* great decisions are made with care, made with conviction, not made with polls...*I believe* in tolerance, not in spite of my faith, but because of it. *I believe* in a God who calls us, not to judge our neighbors, but to love them. *I believe* in grace, because I have seen it; in peace, because I have felt it; in forgiveness, because I needed it. *I believe* true leadership is a process of addition, not an act of division. And *I believe* this will be a tough race, down to the wire."

The Apostle's Creed begins with "I believe in God, the Father almighty, Creator of Heaven and Earth. I believe in Jesus Christ...I believe in the Holy Spirit, the communion of saints, the forgiveness of sins, the resurrection of the body, and the life everlasting. Amen."[240] In addition to replicating structural components and refrains of *The Apostle's Creed*, Bush also mentions the topic of forgiveness, which is an important thematic element of *The Apostle's Creed*.

V) Dominant Metaphors: War, Fathers, Road

In *Metaphors We Live By*, George Lakoff and Mark Johnson trace the rhetorical importance of the war metaphor in modern argument: "Many of the things we do in arguing are partially structured by the concept of war. Though there is no physical battle, there is a verbal battle, and the structure of an argument—attack, defense, counterattack, etc.—reflects this. It is in this sense that the ARGUMENT IS WAR metaphor is one that we live by in this culture..."[241]

As stated above, nomination acceptance speeches must attempt to discredit the opposing party's candidate and viewpoints, which is part of a "war" strategy. The rhetoric in Bush's speech reflects this battle mindset in several ways [italics mine]:

> 1) There is direct allusion to it, e.g.: "Their [*The Democrats*] war room is up and running but we are ready."
>
> 2) Indirectly, verb usage also reflects the submerged metaphor of battle: "We will *seize* the moment of American promise" and "Instead of *seizing* this moment, they [Clinton and Gore] have squandered it." Also: "I will not *attack* a part of this country…"
>
> 3) Bush denies being a part of any past battle, as a Washington outsider: "I don't have enemies *to fight*. I have no stake in the bitter arguments of the last few years."

About halfway through the speech, Bush invokes the image of his father through this statement, which echoes two aspects of Bush, Sr.'s rhetoric in the previous decade: "A time of prosperity is a test of vision. And our nation today needs vision." Political "vision" (or a lack thereof) was a key point for President George Herbert Walker Bush in the early 1990's. Thomas Singer explains this Bush tie to "vision" in the Introduction to *The Vision Thing*: "'The vision thing'—[is] a phrase that [G. H. W.] Bush himself had inadvertently coined early in his administration as a self acknowledged problem of articulating a clear vision for the country…" In 1992, Bush, Sr., had employed the metaphor of the "sunrise of American promise" in one of his key 1992 campaign speeches; this was the same campaign in which Bush, Sr., introduced the image of a "kinder, gentler nation" healed by "a thousand points of light."[242]

Another dominant metaphor in the 2000 George W. Bush speech is "the road/highways/path" allusion which is used four times. Near the halfway point, Bush characterizes America's future as that of the "rising road." He depicts Gore as a roadblock: "It is the sum of his [Gore's] message—the politics of the roadblock, the philosophy of the stop sign."

Bush evokes the image of the "road" as a recurring motif of the speech with a statement near the end: "I am not running in borrowed clothes." In this line, we are given the physical image of Bush "running" while at the same time understanding it as metaphor of "running for office." "Running" works metonymically here; Bush supplies the verb and we are left to conjure the image of something to run on—a road, a path.

About twenty minutes before the ending, Bush calls upon his peers to: "usher in an era of responsibility," implying that the year 2000 and the Clinton/Gore administration was a time of irresponsibility. In the final moments of the speech, Bush states that Americans must "live…on the sunrise side of the mountain." This symbolic phrase is repeated twice in the peroration, giving it added rhetorical value, since it signals the speech's conclusion. The "mountain" is the ending image of the speech; the metaphor of the sunrise is also a callback to his father's 1992 presidential campaign as stated above.

There are myriad rhetorical devices employed by Bush that suggest a "father and son" imagistic link at the archetypal level in his speech:

1) Bush's re-vamping of his father's old expression "the vision thing" as a new line in his own speech, and the use of "sunrise" side of the mountain in his speech as a major metaphor in the peroration links George W. Bush to his father's campaign rhetoric from a decade earlier.

2) There are more allusions to the Paternal in the George W. Bush speech than the Maternal; he aligns himself with the Paternal in a positive way.

3) The speech was delivered in a hall in Philadelphia, Pennsylvania. Bush alludes to Philadelphia twice, once in a direct reference, establishing it as a location of historical importance and the second time, referencing the actual hall, the First Union Center, as a submerged callback which reminds the audience of its historic geographic link to the Founding Fathers [italics mine]: "Our founders first defined that purpose here in *Philadelphia*"; "Tonight, *in this hall*, we resolve to be...not the party of repose..." Philadelphia, as a locus of American history, provides a geographic touchstone that allows Bush to connect his father and his candidacy to George Washington. Thus, in the opening minute of his speech, Bush establishes a rhetorical and archetypal imagistic link to Philadelphia, the Founding Fathers of America, and the Bush political dynasty.

4) Bush alludes to Poet Laureate Robert Frost for a double "father-son" correlation: the line of Frost poetry cited on page eight describes the Founding Fathers, whose highest hope, "as Robert Frost described it, was 'to occupy the land with character.'" R.W. Apple, Jr., writing in *The New York Times*,[243] says that this was also a subtle way to raise the specter of another beloved American president, John F. Kennedy, Jr.: "In a further though more direct thrust at the president he hopes to succeed, the Republican nominee quoted poet Robert Frost, remembered by older Americans for his appearance at John F. Kennedy's inaugural four decades ago."

5) Bush's mention of deceased Lieutenant Governor Bob Bullock, his political mentor, also evokes aspects of a "father-son" pairing, as Molly Ivins points out in the Introduction to *Shrub*.[244]

6) Even Bush's selection of running mate, Richard Cheney as Vice President, could be categorized as part of the father-son complex manifested in Bush's candidacy. Cheney served in the elder Bush's administration, and is older than George W. Bush.

VI) Frequent Constructs with Negators

Bush employed "not" forty times in this speech.[245] It was a major rhetorical style employed in one of his refrains, e.g. "Not this time. Not this year…" About one-third of the way into the speech, it is used in inverted form, coming after verbs [italics mine]: "Tonight, in this hall, we *resolve to be…not* the party of repose but the part of reform. We *will write, not* footnotes, but chapters in the American story."

CORRELATIONS TO THE COMBAT MYTH

Bush establishes a "divine" linkage to the Founding Fathers and his father, George H. W. Bush in the beginning of the speech. He references Gore's status as Vice President (thus locating Gore in the current government) from the start. He aligns himself with the Midland, Texas sky, where he grew up believing: "The sky is the limit." Bush locates himself as a Beltway outsider, a Champion from 'another land' named Texas, where thick accents are just one part of a different outlook where he "accomplished a lot": "I don't have a lot of things that come with Washington," and "Don't mess with Texas."

In the final portions of the speech, Bush alludes to near-defeat for America as a whole: "At times, we lost our way. But we are coming home." He alludes to his own possible defeat near the ending: "I believe this will be a tough race, down to the wire...Their attacks will be relentless, but they will be answered...We are facing something familiar, but they are facing something new." Here, Bush begins to develop the idea of a new "cult" to come, "Compassionate Conservatism," which he says will emerge with Gore's defeat, in that the Republicans are "now the party" of ideas, innovations, idealism, inclusion, simple and powerful hope: "An era of tarnished ideals is giving way to a responsibility era." Because President Clinton and Vice President Gore, as Democrats, were elected from 1992–2000, the Republican agenda would be seen as a "new order" or a cycle change in the 2000 election season.

The structural relationship to the combat myth as detailed by Fontenrose, which uses Apollo's battle with Python as a point of departure into an investigation of the origins of all combat myth in Greek literature[246] was outlined above; the presence of the combat myth in terms of overall purpose is evident here, too. As Burke points out: "If there is to be a combat, it must be fought before our very eyes—otherwise the story-teller has not lived up to the obligations of his trade. Tautologically stated: If a combat myth, then certainly a combat."[247] Gore, as the other combatant, is named directly by Bush, and some political punches are thrown his way in the nomination acceptance speech text.

Another aspect of the combat myth present in the Bush address is related to his use of "not": rhetorical negators. Bush relies on its usage, as previously stated. Burke points out that the use of "the negative" in rhetoric and mythic narrative further signifies the presence of the combat myth, as negatives imply their opposites: "...the peculiarly linguistic marvel, the negative. The negative, as such, offers a basis to think in terms of antitheses (yes-no, good-evil, true-false, right-wrong, order-disorder, cosmos-chaos, success-failure, presence-absence, pleasure-gain, clean-unclean, life-death, love-hate—or, recombining these last two sets, Eros-Thanatos)...*When translated into terms of mythic narrative*, however, *such opposition can become a quasi-temporal 'combat' between the two terms*, with the corresponding possibility that one of the terms can be pictured as 'vanquishing' the other. Or they can be thought of as alternatively uppermost, in periodic or cyclic succession..."[248]

Thus, Bush's speech, replete with the use of "not" (negators) and additionally, the submerged "war metaphors" especially evident in verb usage (as detailed previously, e.g., "We will *seize* the moment of American promise"), leaves the impression for the listener of a rhetorical battle: a struggle between combatants which signifies the metaphoric "killing" of the old order—or in mythological terms, blood purification in order to usher in a new era or the new cult.

CONCLUSION

David L. Miller, in his December 12, 1994, lecture on "Mythopoiesis...Beyond the Postmodern," reminds us that the presidential election cycle and its term limits are a "remnant of agricultural mythology," part of a psychic need to turn the soil in order to ensure seeds will grow into new crops.[249] The combat myth, with its seasonal cyclicity, is another way of "turning"; this can be related to political turns.

George W. Bush became the forty-third President of the United States on January 20, 2001. George W. Bush's 2000 presidential nomination acceptance speech—a representative example of a modern election staple in terms of rhetoric and function—reveals several distinct characteristics when viewed through the dual lens of literary criticism and mythological studies.

Bush's use of two specific refrains ("They have not led. We will." and "It won't be long now.") directly intersects with the combat myth, albeit rhetorically: a verbal challenge to an older administration, a promise of coming change with the new. The two *ad libs* in the speech were related to protocol and emphasis. Through both statements and jokes, Bush linked himself to the Founding Fathers, and his own father, a former president, thus establishing himself as a sort of "American royalty" in terms of lineage; this could be seen as aspiring to a celestial plane, or as an attempt to reclaim the celestial plane in terms of American symbolism and family heritage. His unfinished anecdote involving disenfranchised members of society serves to locate Bush as a person of privilege ("a white man in a suit") but also as self-aware of his privileged status. This part of the narrative, however, is without resolution; this thread of the story is left unfinished.

Aspects of Christianity were represented in the speech, through liturgy and metonymy; this could also be seen as part of a "new order" forecast by Bush, with the 2000 campaign promise of "compassionate conservatism." The dominant metaphors of war, the road, the sunrise side of the mountain, and "the father" also intersect points of the combat myth. War does so directly, through rhetoric: the fight of the campaign. The road symbolizes the hero's journey, and also that of the act of "running" for office. The "sunrise side of the mountain," in addition to a tie to his father's previous symbolic use of "dawn" imagery, highlights the mountain, a celestial mythical place of import, where one may touch the heavens. The father-son construction so prevalent in the speech could also be construed as related to the "younger" Bush challenging the "older" Bush in terms of family cosmology, or in other words, another iteration of the combat myth with a familial focus. And finally, the use of negators, a "No! Not this!" rhetorical flourish, is inherent to the combat myth structure; the opposition is direct, the fight immediate, the outcome to be determined.

The combat myth is reenacted rhetorically and symbolically in the modern American political landscape through presidential elections. But there is another aspect of intersection with the Apollo-Python myth to keep in mind here. The Oracle at Delphi was a place where the future was foretold. A presidential nominee must make promises of the future as well; it is another way "to see the future"—of the changes the new leader/hero will promise to bring about, or "the vision thing." Perhaps there is a further connection to American presidential elections to be explored here "post-combat," when the new "cult" is established, and the future is foretold. Are visions of the future, from the psyche's standpoint, needed throughout presidential political campaigns, and even post-victory? Nominee Bush states in his 2000 speech: "And our nation today needs a vision." The ability to "forecast the future" is seemingly part of the nominee's mission. The psychic Delphic link or prognosticative tie to the Python: does it remain as part of the winner's governance, post-Victory? Is the Delphic, "seeing the future" link always part of the Combat Myth, especially when applied to politics?

We can end our examination with Fontenrose's description of the Victory step, since it compares directly to the presidential inauguration, a reward for facing the dragon: "He celebrated his victory with a banquet and other festivities. He was cheered by gods and men."[250]

Works Cited

Apple, R.W., Jr. "The Republicans—The Overview…" 4 August 2000.
The New York Times. Accessed 23 August 2011.
  http://www.nytimes.com/2000/08/04/us/republicans-overview-bush-accepting-gop-nomination-pledges-use-these-good-times.html.

"*Apostle's Creed.*" Wikipedia.org.
http://en.wikipedia.org/wiki/Apostles'_Creed
Accessed 23 August 2011.

Burke, Kenneth. "Myth, Poetry and Philosophy." *Theories of Myth*, Robert A. Segal, ed. New York: Garland, 1996. 11-35.

Bush, George W. "And It Won't Be Long Now." *Los Angeles Times*, August 4, 2000. GOP Nomination Acceptance Speech Transcript. Philadelphia, PA: August 4, 2000. *Los Angeles Times.* http://articles.latimes.com/2000/aug/04/news/mn-64431.

Campbell, James. E. *The American Campaign: U.S. Presidential Campaigns and the National Vote*. College Station, TX: Texas A & M UP, 2000.

Chevalier, Jean and Alain Gheerbrant. *A Dictionary of Symbols.* Trans. by John Buchanan-Brown. Oxford: Blackwell, 1994.

Fontenrose, Joseph. *Python: A Study of Delphic Myth and Its Origins.* New York: Biblo and Tannen, 1974.

Ivins, Molly. *Shrub.* New York: Vintage, 2000.

Kang, K. Connie. "Across the globe, Christians are united by *Lord's Prayer.*" *Los Angeles Times*, p. A13. April 8, 2007.

Kristeva, Julia. *Language the Unknown: An Initiation into Linguistics.* Trans. Anne M. Menke. New York: Columbia UP, 1989.

Kugler, Paul. *The Alchemy of Discourse.* London: Bucknell UP, 1982.

Lakoff, George and Mark Johnson. *Metaphors We Live By.* Chicago: U of Chicago P, 1980.

"*The Lord's Prayer.*" Wikipedia.org. Accessed 20 February 2012. http://en.wikipedia.org/wiki/The_Lord's_Prayer.

Miller, David L. "Mythopoiesis…Beyond the Postmodern." Myth Lecture. 12 December, 1994. Pacifica Graduate Institute, Santa Barbara, California.

Miller, David L. *The New Polytheism.* Dallas: Spring, 1981.

Minot, Stephen. *Three Genres.* Upper Saddle River, N.J.: Prentice Hall, 1998.

Quinion, Michael. Editor, Worldwidewords.org. E-mail to author. 6 December 2000.

Singer, Tom. "Introduction: The Vision Thing." *The Vision Thing: Myth, Politics and Psyche in the World.* London: Routledge, 2000.

---

[220] Kristeva, p. 282.
[221] Campbell [James], p. 141.
[222] Campbell [James], p. 146.
[223] It is an especially important speech for a candidate who challenges an incumbent candidate, party, or administration. For example, in 2012, the GOP candidate faces the incumbent, or established administration of President Barack Obama.
[224] The minutes or timing as reported in *The New York Daily News*: http://articles.nydailynews.com/2000-08-04/news/18148422_1_barbara-bush-risky-anti-candle-scheme-moment-of-american-promise. For the full text of the 2000 George W. Bush nomination acceptance speech as analyzed in this essay: http://articles.latimes.com/2000/aug/04/news/mn-64431.
[225] Quinion.
[226] Fontenrose, p. 1.
[227] Fontenrose, p. 2.
[228] Chevalier and Gheerbrant, p. 779.
[229] Fontenrose, p. 465.
[230] Burke, p. 12.
[231] Burke, p. 13.
[232] Fontenrose, pps. 9-11/Burke, p. 13.
[233] Burke, p. 16.
[234] Burke, p. 25.
[235] Burke, p. 23.
[236] Burke, pps. 23-24.
[237] Burke, p. 19.
[238] Kugler, p. 63.
[239] *The Lord's Prayer* is recognized by billions worldwide. On Easter Sunday, 2007, for example, it was estimated that 2 billion people across the globe said or sang it (Kang).
[240] "Apostle's Creed." Wikipedia.org. 4 Feb. 2012. http://en.wikipedia.org/wiki/Apostles'_Creed.
[241] Lakoff and Johnson, p. 4.
[242] Singer, p. 1.
[243] Apple, R.W. "The Republicans—The Overview."

[244] Ivins, p. xiv.
[245] Both of the two main candidates used "not" frequently in their 2000 nomination acceptance speeches. Vice President Al Gore, who was part of the two-term Clinton-Gore administration, used "not" thirty-four times in his 2000 nomination acceptance speech. Gore's speech was longer than Bush's speech by 1,368 words.
[246] Burke, p. 284.
[247] Burke, p. 287.
[248] Burke 288-289.
[249] In *The New Polytheism*, David L. Miller writes: "There is an incipient polytheism always lurking in democracy. This polytheism will surface during the history of democracies if the civilization does not first succumb to anarchy. In calling our time polytheist, we are saying something about the state of democracy in our time" (26).
[250] Fontenrose, p. 11.

21) A Few Thoughts On Adaptation

(*Note: This essay is different from the others in this collection; it's a "how to" instruction. Through the years, I've taught myth and fairy tale adaptation at a number of universities and workshops.*[251] *Often, I'm asked if I can provide something like a workbook for participants to keep—something more than handouts. As a writer who has sat through many writing workshops and classes, I understand that request. A long PowerPoint lecture ends, and then you, as writer, must complete the major part of the task at hand on your own. Help! It's quite daunting to complete months or years of work on a creative-adaptation process, writing hundreds of pages, with only your handwritten notes and a few class sheets. I've written the essay below for a specific audience: creative writers interested in myth or fairy tale adaptation. But I hope it's of interest to others as well. The essay could be seen as an "insider's view" or a "deconstructive" look at the process of mythopoesis. It is published for the first time here, although I have given versions of this lecture in public many times.*)

> "And this is the mythic space I think we are talking about today when we think or say 'myth.' We are talking about a creative space of the imagination where we begin to think with a tradition of re-visioning myth poetically. That isn't going to produce a poem necessarily. Arriving here will have produced a way of seeing. And this will be a way of seeing anything. Call this a poetic seeing of the metaphor." –Stephanie Pope, "Mythopoesis in the Twenty-First Century or 'Poetry in the Extreme.'"[252]

Each year, stories from myths and folklore are adapted for poems, film, theater and fiction. Many of these are financial blockbusters, and are admired; sometimes they are so popular that the adaptations carry from one form to another, such as a myth-related novel adapted to film. The written forms of myth and folklore evolved from oral traditions, and movies are the newest way for storytellers to share and interpret these tales of wonder and marvel. But how do you adapt or update a myth or fairy tale in any genre for a contemporary audience—and ensure it can exhibit its psychological and symbolic import, to work its magic?

Some of the most acclaimed filmmakers today are drawn to classic subject matter; they adapt and reinvent. In *The Mythology of Star Wars*, acclaimed journalist Bill Moyers interviews George Lucas about his use of myth, and about the influence of his mentor, mythologist Joseph Campbell: "Well, when I did *Star Wars*, I consciously set about to recreate myths. And the classic mythological motifs. And I wanted to use those motifs to deal with issues that existed today."[253] Director-writer-producer Tim Burton says: "I've always loved the idea of fairy tales…What interests me is taking those classic images and themes and trying to contemporize them a bit. I believe folk tales and fairy tales have some sort of psychological foundation that makes that possible."[254]

Filmmaker Guillermo del Toro says, in a Q & A quoted in *The Portland Mercury* in 2010: "I think everything I write is a fairy tale, to a degree."[255] Del Toro also states: "That's what I love about fairy tales; they tell the truth…"[256]

From the *Harry Potter* series to *Avatar,* modern literature and films pulse with characters, plotlines and symbols inspired by myth and fairy tales. As Joseph Campbell famously observes in *The Hero With a Thousand Faces* (1949): "The latest incarnation of Oedipus, the continued romance of Beauty and the Beast, stand this afternoon on the corner of 42nd Street and Fifth Avenue, waiting for the traffic light to change."[257]

For adaptation, the use of myth and fairy tales can be divided into three categories in terms of creative writing and "setting":

1) **CLASSICAL**—Adaptations set in "classical periods" like the films *Clash of the Titans*, *Troy*, and *Immortals* or novelist David Malouf's *Ransom*.

2) **UPDATES**—Adaptations set in more modern times, like *O Brother, Where Art Thou?*, *Enchanted*, *The Princess and the Frog*, Sarah Ruhl's play *Eurydice*, Luis Alfaro's play *Oedipus El Rey*, or the novel *Beastly* by Alex Finn, and its subsequent movie.

3) **HYBRIDS**—These are projects with some elements adapted from myth or fairy tales that are used in a modern parallel or to create a unique, magical world. The end result may maintain aspects of "classical," "magical," and "modern"; mythic or folkloric elements are actively in use, and/or several tales may be combined. Movies in the *Harry Potter* series, *Thor*, *Tangled*, *Star Wars*, *Avatar*, *Pan's Labyrinth*, *Shrek*, and *Percy Jackson and the Lightning Thief* are "hybrids." Some of the movies listed above (e.g., *Harry Potter*, *Shrek*, and *Percy Jackson*) are based on very popular books for children and young adults, and those authors have successfully re-imagined myth and fairy tale elements from a modern viewpoint.

Like most readers and viewers, I encountered myth and fairy tales when I was young. I don't remember how old I was when my parents first read a fairy tale to me. But I have a distinct memory as a nine year-old of staring at a framed map of "The Marvelous Land of Oz, Drawn by Prof. Wogglebug T. E." in a children's section of a small town library in Oklahoma, and thinking it was surely the most wonderful thing I'd ever seen in my life. As a young reader, I explored L. Frank Baum's unique Oz world of "American fairy tales," checking out all the volumes in the Oz series from the library as quickly as I could read them. I loved J.R.R. Tolkien's *The Hobbit* and *The Lord of the Rings*. Many of us have fond childhood recollections of being introduced to magical literary realms that captivated our imaginations. A recent generation has grown up appreciating J.K. Rowling's amazing *Harry Potter* series as readers, and then experiencing a decade of wonder and awe as filmgoers—they read all the books and then saw all of the movies. For legions of Hogwarts fans, this fantastic experience extended well past childhood, through adolescence, and into adulthood. As a university instructor, I have witnessed firsthand the passion and enthusiasm of *Harry Potter* devotees who, having grown up with the books and movies, lobbied as college students for the inclusion of those books to be part of a dramatic writing adaptation course curriculum. They simply could not get enough of them; they wanted to analyze and deconstruct them, too.

Why do magical tales generate such enthusiasm and devotion? Why do legends of extraordinary worlds enchant us so? Why do they matter? In the early days of psychology, Sigmund Freud and Carl Jung wrote extensively about the value of myth and fairy tales to the psyche, exploring theories about dreams and the patterns of human behavior reflected back to us through these special stories. Bruno Bettelheim, in the introduction to his famous work *The Uses of Enchantment*, reminds us that fairy tales, in all their complexities, illustrate life's meaning in multivalent ways which may be appreciated by both children and adults: "If we hope to live not just from moment to moment, but in true consciousness of our existence, then our greatest need and most difficult achievement is to find meaning in our lives…at each age we seek, and must be able to find, some modicum of meaning congruent with how our minds and understanding have already developed."[258]

In addition to pointing us towards wisdom about humanity and the meaning of life, author Maria Tatar, Chair of Folklore and Mythology at Harvard University, explains that fairy tales last because they entertain. Tatar says that the cultural resilience of fairy tales is incontestable: "Fairy tales, as folklorists and historians never tire of reminding us, have their roots in a peasant culture relatively uninhibited in its expressive energy. For centuries, farm laborers and household workers relied on the telling of tales to shorten the hours devoted to repetitive harvesting tasks and domestic chores."[259] Tasks were completed while fairy tales were told; workers were entertained, perhaps even inspired by the tales.

The word "entertain" derives from the French "entretenir" and the Late Latin "intertenere," which means to hold "mutually intertwined"—as in to hold us in an imaginary world.[260] The phrase and concept of "Once upon a time" have been in use in English since 1380, according to the *Oxford English Dictionary*, when a tale was begun with: "Onsy...oppon a day."[261] The phrase signals that the tale we're about to encounter, no matter when it is set, is relevant, universal and timeless.

English poet and playwright William Shakespeare exhibited a vast knowledge of mythology and of the fairy world in his plays and poems.[262] Shakespeare is known as the greatest writer in the English language. Wikipedia lists Shakespeare as the Number One bestselling fiction writer to this day.[263] The bard utilized aspects of fantasy and magic in plays like *A Midsummer Night's Dream, The Tempest,* and *Macbeth*. Shakespeare's use of supernatural and fairy worlds both enchants and terrifies us, depending on the genre. Scholars point to Shakespeare's grasp of Ovid and Virgil as vital to his work. In addition to mythic and fairy-world characters, the bard used hundreds of mythic allusions in his plays and poems. Obviously, Shakespeare was invested in the power of myth and fairy stories. Could Shakespeare's powerful use of myth and folklore contribute to making his work so viable today in the modern world? It's interesting to consider.

For a contemporary myth or fairy tale adaptation to "work," it's vital to acknowledge and honor the value of each individual myth or tale. In other words, although there may be ways in which some myths and tales are similar (e.g., in structure, archetype or motif), for the adaptation process, it's best to see each tale as unique, as its own *sui generis* template.

Before the adaptation process is explained, it's crucial to explore some basic ideas about myths and fairy tales. What exactly is a myth? What is a fairy tale? Scholars have been debating the definition of each for centuries.

MYTH

In our contemporary sound-byte culture, the word "myth" is often used interchangeably with the word "lie." For example, you might hear someone complaining about "The Myth of Democracy" on a television news show or on a blog, implying that democracy doesn't exist. This usage of "myth," as a synonym for falsehood, is not helpful to storytellers.

A myth constitutes something that is so true that it has withstood the test of time, and has survived through thousands of years. It is a sacred story, passed on in oral tradition, and then later collected or written down. A myth may feature gods and goddesses who were worshipped in temples and at altars in days when polytheism was predominant; or a myth may describe the creation of the cosmos and of a people. A myth may track the initiation of a hero, or a heroine's trial. A myth is usually part of an elaborate system of stories (as in the connections and intersections between the myths from the Greek pantheon, for example). Scholars have observed that myths show us the boundaries and taboos of human behavior, and of the human imagination. In the twentieth century (and before), there was considerable debate among scholars about the connection between myth and ritual. Although no one knows for sure which came first (myth or ritual), we do know that in some traditions they are deeply fused.

In *Icanchu's Drum*, scholar Lawrence Sullivan writes: "Myth does not simply denote a species of narrative; literary or oral genres are only symptoms of myth. Myth is not a form of lore but a *quality of imaginal existence*. Myth is the imagination beholding its own reality and plumbing the source of its own creativity as it relates to creativity in every form (plant and planetary life, animal fertility, intelligence, art). Myth reveals the sacred foundations and religious character of the imagination. Mythic symbols signify the possibility, variety, and meaning of cultural imagery."[264] Every creative writer wishes to bring us a quality of imaginal existence in her or his writing.

Myths are powerful because they reflect back to us who we are, and who we've always been. In *Parallel Myths*, J.F. Bierlein writes: "Myth is an eternal mirror in which we see ourselves...Myth has something to say to everyone, as it has something to say about everyone."[265] There is a universal aspect to myth that, when activated, enables writers and filmmakers to reach nearly everyone who encounters his or her work.

If it is true that myths are storehouses of images and patterns of human behavior, then myths may also be predictive. What will happen next? What happened previously? A myth can show you. William Doty writes: "Here we see that myths guide understandings of the past—of the traditional—*and they anticipate the future*. Each mythic grasping of meaning contributes to significances yet to come, and determines where a society sets its horizons and its limits as to what it considers 'truly human.' Myths both convey the most important ways to be 'successful' members of society and teach the permitted parameters of behavior that only certain individuals (priests and rulers, artists and musicians, and today, athletes and the very rich) may exceed without penalty. Myths fund moral codes, philosophies and theologies."[266] For filmmakers and creative writers, this is essential terrain. Whether you are adapting a specific myth or creating a hybrid world inspired by various folk tales, you are creating codes of behaviors and establishing boundaries: the possibilities of action.

Mircea Eliade, one of the most renowned scholars of myth and religion of the twentieth century, states that myth "relates an event that took place in primordial Time, the time of the 'beginnings.' In other words, myth tells us how, through the deeds of a Supernatural Being, a reality came into existence..."[267] Myth is generative, at the root of creation, the key to creating reality. In this sense, every film creates its own mythic reality.

FAIRY TALE

By and large, the gods and goddesses are often absent from what we recognize today as fairy tales. The term "fairy tale" or "conte de fée" was coined in the seventeenth century by French writer Madame D'Aulnoy, otherwise known as Marie-Catherine Le Jumel de Barneville.[268] Some folklorists prefer the German term "Märchen" or "wonder tale." Tatar provides context for the phrase in *The Hard Facts of the Grimms' Fairy Tales*: "The term fairy tale, by contrast, has been associated with both oral and literary traditions but above all is reserved for narratives set in a fictional world where preternatural events and supernatural intervention are wholly taken for granted."[269]

To be absolutely correct from an academic perspective, the term "fairy tale" is categorized generally as "folklore," but is different than a folk tale. The folk tale, per se, usually has a more naturalistic setting than a fairy tale, which is associated with fantasy; the folk tale may represent customs of a certain community or people.

The fairy tale is a distinct genre within folklore, but there is still discussion in the field about its definition. Stith Thompson, perhaps best known for his contribution to the Aarne-Thompson classification system of folklore, suggests in *The Folktale* that fairies are not at all necessary to fairy tales—and you'd be more likely to find magic and talking animals than fairies in most of them.[270]

Eliade notes, in his essay "Myths and Fairy Tales," that folklore is often classified as merely for children or as a "literature of diversion."[271] But Jack Zipes, in *Fairy Tales as Myth: Myth as Fairy Tale* contends that Eliade believed that fairy tales are sacred vessels—and express "mythic notions and motifs that are camouflaged" in the tales.[272] Why is this important for creative writers and filmmakers? Because fairy tales resonate with the psyche as well; they have powerful themes, characters and symbols that deserve careful "updates" (used here to mean a conceptual, cultural modern translation) in the adaptation process, just as myths require.

And if you are interested in actual fairies as characters, you will tap into a timeless story with "spiritual" possibilities. Folklore authority Katharine Briggs traces belief in fairies to "almost to the verge of prehistory" and finds written evidence of these beliefs in medieval times.[273] The enchantress Morgan Le Fay's name, from Thomas Malory's 1485 *Le Morte D'Arthur*, is considered an early use of the word ("Le Fay"), related to mortal women with magical powers. The etymology of "fairy" references the three famous "Fates," or Italian "fatae," who came to visit upon a child's birth to predict his or her fate. In Brigg's *An Encyclopedia of Fairies*, she notes: "'Fairy' originally meant 'fai-erie,' a state of enchantment."[274]

ADAPTATION PROCESS FOR WRITERS

I) SOURCES

The first issue that adapters face is finding the right story. How do you find a myth or fairy tale to adapt? What are the key sources? Two recommendations are:

>1). Read.

>2). Think back to the stories you loved as a child. What were your favorite stories in childhood? It's best to read myths and tales directly from classical authors, myth dictionaries, folklore collections, and other myth/folklore reference materials (such as Stith Thompson's *Motif-Index of Folk-Literature: A Classification of Narrative Elements in Folk Tales, Ballads, Myths, Fables, Mediaeval Romances, Exempla, Fabliaux, Jestbooks, and Local Legends*). A word of caution: One of the most important legal points involved with myth/fairy tale adaptation is that you must only adapt a translation of a myth or fairy tale that is in public domain. Translations are copyrighted and the work of the translator is protected.

There is an old saying among myth and fairy tale adapters: you don't find the myth or fairy tale; it finds you. There is most likely some truth to that, as you will definitely discover things about yourself as you work on the tale you choose to adapt. This also points to following one's intuition about which story to work with, as that could be a sign of attraction to the tale from an unconscious perspective. I also think that the seeds of theme may be rooted in any intuition about a story you choose to adapt.

IMAGERY AND ARCHETYPAL PLANES

As you choose your tale to adapt, it's important to have two other concepts in mind: the power of imagery and the concept of archetypal planes. In 2006, Maggie Macary, on the Daily Arrows blog, wrote: "An image is a weave of subtleties that encompass texture, emotion, content. An image is not what we look at; it is what we see through, as seeing through a lens or a mirror. It has the ability to change us, emotionally, psychologically, perhaps even spiritually. It gives us emotion and context and supplies us with the textures of the world around us."[275] Macary's points are especially pertinent to myth and fairy tale images and their psychic resonance. This is something for all those interested in adaptation to consider, and it may affect your choice of a tale when you "see" a story "through" its images.

Another valuable tool important to consider when adapting are the different levels of archetypal "planes" that a story may offer. This can be very useful when trying to visualize a film for a storyboard, but it has value even as inspiration for writing. There are three key locations that I recommend to help a story "honor its magic":

> 1). The celestial plane. This is the plane of the heavens, the divine. What action in the myth or fairy tale you choose takes place in the celestial plane? In Greek myth, this plane is sometimes represented as "Mount Olympus" where the gods and goddesses are. In fairy tales, sometimes this level is the "royal" one, which occurs in the castle, as mountains and castles touch the sky, close to the ether of eternity. This is an "above" level.

2). The earthly plane. This is the mortal plane, the plane where humans, for the most part, reside. This could be thought of as the "ordinary" or "everyday" plane.

3) The underworld plane. From a mythological perspective, this is a "below" level. In some traditions, it is equivalent to "hell," but in others, it may be a place for souls to go after death. Some traditions hold that it is the place where life begins, e.g. a seed grows from below. It can also be associated with "taboo" or shadow enterprises outside of "public life," such as the word's modern use in describing clandestine crime. In adapting myth and fairy tales, an underworld level is important; "descent" and "ascent" are often key to action sequences in a story, especially as related to a hero's arc,[276] and if there is an "underworld" plane, it makes this possible.

Again, my recommendation is to try to have all three planes represented in the adaptation, metaphorically or otherwise, to ensure the most movement between archetypal planes; this helps to give an adaptation more "magic."

II) RESEARCH

Through the years, I've found that this next piece of advice seems to be the one that people find most surprising: Gather as many versions of the stories/myths/fairy tales as possible, preferably 3–7 versions of your myth from a wide range of mythological sources. Document and list the stories or folk accounts chronologically, so that you can refer to them easily for analysis. Different mythographers, folklorists and writers report variations as each retell the same story; different epochs and cultures imprint these stories, too. Note any important rites or rituals connected to the tale; these can also be a clue towards "theme" and "character development."

Charting versions of tales in this way will enable you to track the central characters, symbols, plots, setting, and themes related to the story, through time.

A) Archetypes: Characters. Who is the tale about? Who does the action involve? Who tells the story? Who changes in it? Images of archetypes or characters are very helpful to inspire character development in adaptation. If you are writing about classical figures, go to a museum with a classical art collection (or access it online). This is highly recommended for inspiration. Visualizing a character helps to understand it in greater detail; visualization helps especially in terms of updating personal props related to characters. Does your key character or archetype have an "ally?" How does this ally help to define your central character?

B) Symbols. What are the leading symbols in your story? What are the iconic "props" that your central characters use? If you are doing an "update," it is necessary to update or "translate" the major symbols for a contemporary audience. This is also related to Setting (see D below). Both A and B are linked to the definition of image, as well.

C) Plot. List the major story steps of the myth or fairy tale. Boil the plot down to an outline of action beats, based upon the various versions you've read. If you read multiple versions of the myth or fairy tale, you'll have a firmer idea of what the plot essentials are, through time, and which ones you are most eager to "write through," the ones that resonate the most with your own goals or thematic choice. Any good plot should bring rising conflict and produce change, but with an adaptation, and several different versions of stories to choose from through the ages, you can make informed choices about plot steps.

D) Setting. The setting should reflect what the story dictates, but setting, too, may be highly symbolic and "interpretative" in an adaptation. Keep in mind the three archetypal planes, as settings for scenes are decided. Some settings may be "updated" metaphorically, depending on the tale and adaptation style.

E) Theme (Psychological Function). What is the story is about? What is its point? This is the "arena" of theme. Do you see the myth or tale differently than others do? If so, explore what you see in the story versus what you think is a more "accepted" interpretation. What is the psychological function of the story? What does it say to or about humanity? Why has the story remained "of interest" for so many years? If the story has fallen out of favor, why do you think so? These are the types of questions that help writers find a working theme in myth and fairy tale adaptation.

F) Transformation. Who changes? What changes? Many myths and folk tales have magical transformations in them. What is magical about the tale you are adapting? What is the source of its magic? How is the world of the story different after "magic" happens? How is magic related to the function of transformation specifically in the tale you've chosen to adapt? Has this function changed in various versions of the tale you've chosen, through time?

These are the beginning steps needed to work on a myth or fairy tale adaptation as a writer or filmmaker. Writing sometimes feels like an alchemical process; through the creative journey, our lead turns to gold and we don't know how or why, but it happens in the "doing" of it. Adapting a myth or fairy tale is a psychic and creative adventure; it reflects something back to us about ourselves—its own hidden treasure to be uncovered in the creative act. A good adaptation adds to current culture something of value, too. The best way to experience it is to begin.

---

[251] These include courses at Pepperdine University (Creative Writing and Screenwriting), University of Southern California (School of Theatre), UCLA Extension Writers Program, Hollins University's MFA Screenwriting Program, and individual talks/workshops, such as in the Drama Department of Catholic University, the Writer's Center (Bethesda, MD), the Los Angeles Women's Theatre Project, and the 2011 Dramatists Guild National Conference, held at George Mason University.
[252] Stephanie Pope, "Mythopoesis in the Twenty-First Century or 'Poetry in the Extreme'" 2 January 2012. *Mythopoetry Scholar: Annual Reflections in Depth Psychology*, Volume 3.
http://www.mythopoetry.com/mythopoetics/sch12_pope_mythopoesis.html.
[253] George Lucas. "The Mythology of Star Wars with George Lucas and Bill Moyers," FFH, 1999. Films for the Humanities and Science. Produced and Directed by Pamela Mason Wagner.
[254] Tim Burton. "Bio."Internet Movie Database.com.
http://www.imdb.com/name/nm0000318/bio.
[255] Guillermo del Toro. Quote #1: *Portland Mercury*, 30 September 2010.
http://blogtown.portlandmercury.com/BlogtownPDX/archives/2010/09/30/a-few-notes-on-guillermo-del-toros-qanda.
[256] Guillermo del Toro. Quote #2: "Bio." Internet Movie Database.com.
http://www.imdb.com/name/nm0868219/bio.
[257] Joseph Campbell, *The Hero With a Thousand Faces*. Novato, CA: New World Library, 2008, 3rd edition, p. 2. (Original edition copyrighted 1949 by Bollingen Books and published by Pantheon Books.)

[258] Bruno Bettelheim, *The Uses of Enchantment*, New York: Vintage Books, 2010, p. 3. (Original edition published in 1976 by Alfred A. Knopf.)
[259] Maria Tatar, ed. *The Classic Fairy Tales*, New York: Norton and Co., 1999. "Introduction: Little Red Riding Hood," p. 3.
[260] "Entertain." *Oxford English Dictionary*. 5 February 2012. http://dictionary.oed.com/cgi/entry/50076190?query_type=word&queryword=entertain&first=1&max_to_show=10&sort_type=alpha&result_place=2&search_id=Qtkz-vKtxPF-4500&hilite=50076190. For more on this, please see "Entertainment: The Meaning of the Word and Ritual" in this volume.
[261] "Once." *Oxford English Dictionary*. 5 Feb. 2012. http://dictionary.oed.com/cgi/entry/00331779/00331779se2?query_type=word&queryword=%22Once+Upon+A+Time%22&first=1&max_to_show=10&sort_type=alpha&result_place=1&search_id=EDH0-qh9MNc-13216&hilite=00331779se2.
[262] I write more about Shakespeare's use and knowledge of myth in my monograph: *"We Three": The Mythology of Shakespeare's Weird Sisters*. New York: Peter Lang USA, 2007. See, for example, p. 35.
[263] http://en.wikipedia.org/wiki/List_of_best-selling_fiction_authors. (In fairness, this entry also states it is an incomplete list, as it is impossible to track the sales of many older works.)
[264] From Lawrence Sullivan. *Icanchu's Drum: an Orientation to Meaning in South American Religions* (New York: Macmillan, 1990), p. 22.
[265] J.F. Bierlein. *Parallel Myths*. New York: Ballantine Wellspring (Random House Publshing Group), 1994, p. xiii.
[266] William Doty. "Exploring the Manifold Spheres of Mythos," p. 16. From *Mythosphere*, Volume 1, 2000. *Mythosphere: A Journal for Image, Myth, and Symbol*. 1:2, pps. 115-130.
[267] Mircea Eliade, *Myth and Reality*. Trans. Willard R. Trask. Prospect Heights, IL: Waveland Press, Inc., 1963. Page 5.
[268] Madame Aulnoy and "fairy tale." Jack Zipes, *The Great Fairy Tale Tradition: From Straparola and Basile to the Brothers Grimm*. New York: Norton, 2001, p. 858.
[269] Maria Tatar. *The Hard Facts of the Grimms' Fairy Tales*. Princeton, NJ: Princeton University Press, 1987 & 2003, p. 33.
[270] Stith Thompson, *The Folktale*. Los Angeles: University of California Press, 1977, p. 55.
[271] Mircea Eliade, *Myth and Reality*. Trans. Willard R. Trask. Prospect Heights, IL: Waveland Press, Inc., 1963. "Myth and Fairy Tales," p. 201.
[272] Jack Zipes. *Fairy Tales as Myth: Myth as Fairy Tales*. Lexington, KY: The University Press of Kentucky, 1994, p. 2.

[273] Katharine Briggs. *The Fairies in Tradition and Literature*. London: Routledge, 1967, p. 4.
[274] Katharine Briggs. *An Encyclopedia of Fairies*. New York: Pantheon Books, 1976, p. xi.
[275] Macary, Maggie. "Poetic Basis of Mind: A Lens Into the Imaginal," *Daily Arrows* blog March 8, 2006, republished at: http://www.mythopoetry.com/mythopoetics/essay_myth_imaginal.html. Accessed 29 Aug. 2011.
[276] This is especially true when writing a female protagonist. See *The Heroine's Journey* by Maureen Murdock for more on "descent to the underworld" for heroines.

22) Swimming In the Tweet Stream

(Note: This essay is published for the first time in this volume.)

In ancient times, mythology spread through word of mouth, trade routes (often over water), and through geographic relocation or migration. Is today's tweet stream or timeline (the flow of information feed on social media) comparable to yesterday's trade routes in terms of myth transmission in terms of function? Twitter's[277] stream could be seen as a modern day equivalent to "word of mouth"; a Twitter user communicates thoughts as an individual, addressing others, via the social media network.

Although accounts are free, Twitter is a commercial enterprise; products and services are advertised constantly in its "flow." Social media advertising has replaced older advertising paradigms for corporations, such as surveys and direct marketing. Twitter is a virtual, streaming marketplace—a mix of product, ideas, spam, and personal SMS-like messaging.

In *Approaches to Media Literacy: A Handbook*, co-authors Art Silverblatt, Jane Ferry and Barbara Sinan write: "Today, the oral tradition—the primary source for passing myths from generation to generation—has nearly disappeared. In this vacuum, the media have emerged as primary channels for the transmission of myth."[278] As a social network, Twitter is a form of media. Twitter began in 2006 and as of this writing has 200 million users worldwide.[279] It could be argued that every "tweet" or message on Twitter could be correlated to an aspect of identity and storytelling, and thus is related to myth transmission in purpose and function. Twitter began with asking users to answer one question: "What are you doing?" In 2009, the official Twitter question was changed to: "What's happening?"[280] Another popular slogan related to Twitter is "You are what you tweet."[281]

The possibility for meme[282] virality on Twitter, or "content echo," factors into its story or myth transmission capability; there is a "retweet" or "RT" function that instantly sends out or replicates a copy of another's tweet with a push of a widget. The "retweet" function could be seen as related to a modern concept of retelling—a necessity to the impact of a tale—a way to keep it alive and "in the current."

Marshall McLuhan famously writes that the medium is the message: "And in the long run, for such media or macro-myths such as the phonetic alphabet, printing, photography, the movie, the telegraph, radio, and television, the social action of these forms is also, in the fullest sense, their message or meaning."[283] In 1960, McLuhan notes that we are in a post-literate time, and have passed from "the mechanistic age into the electronic."[284] In *The Art of Immersion*, Frank Rose gives a twenty-first century assessment: "…Mass media are now in decline. The Internet has us focused not on alienation. If anything, people worry that they're too connected for their own good."[285] Rose states that the way to gain followers on Twitter is "by relating information—a process that often involves telling a story."[286] If the medium is the message in regards to story and its transmission, on Twitter this pinpoints the importance of connecting through brevity—as one is limited to using only 140 characters at a time. In other words: concision and image. Rose traces the links between sharing stories and creating a sense of a like-minded community. "When we share stories, we strengthen our links to other people. Within a group…stories establish norms and articulate a defining myth."[287] This correlates to a societal-boundary function of mythology, as myths describe human behavior, including highlights and taboos. Rose says that we now live in a time of "hyperconnectivity," an era whose consequences are still unfolding.[288] Hyperconnectivity suggests that we share more about our lives (our identities) and our stories than ever before.

Larry Carlat, a former Twitter user, writes about how Twitter ruined his life. His essay "Confessions of a Tweeter,"[289] published in *The New York Times* in 2011, seems directly related to the "performative" aspect of social media, somewhat similar to the climax of a ritual or of a performer's expectation of applause at the end of a performance. Carlat, who at one time had 25,000 followers on Twitter,[290] says: "Soon my entire life revolved around tweeting. I stopped reading, rarely listened to music or watched TV. When I was out with friends, I would duck into the bathroom with my iPhone. I tweeted while driving, between sets of tennis, even at the movies." When he wasn't signed on, Carlat found himself composing "faux aphorisms" to send out to his followers later. Carlat states that he began to think and talk that way, too: in 140 characters. Moreover, he says: "But for me, every tweet was a performance."[291] Eventually, after quitting his job (due in part to a complication involving a corporate human resources policy about social media) and a change in his marital status that provoked a tweet that offended his son, Carlat left Twitter. In terms of changing the way the mind works (performing for an audience, changing his thought process, thinking in "bytes," telling his "story" to the world as much as once an hour), Carlat is not alone. Another study says that our attention spans have dropped from twelve minutes in 2001 to five minutes, in 2011, due to social media usage.[292] Does the shorthand of modern tweeting and texting somehow correlate to an aspect of contemporary "myth transmission?" Have mythemes become memes transmittable on social media and smart phones?

Jungian researcher and therapist Charlie Arthur, Twitter user "@Numinousviews," writes: "Twitter is such a great expression of the collective unconscious, so much more so than the mainstream media."[293] Extrapolating from Arthur's idea, perhaps we do experience something of myth, identity, archetypes, numinosity, and the *animus mundi* in the social media stream: iterations and echoes, synchronicity and shadows. Swimming in the tweet stream, we see our own reflections and sometimes we even RT them.

Certainly, fluid storytelling in social media as a way of establishing identity is not exactly the same thing as myth transmission. They are not interchangeable. But it is time to raise questions and wonder about: the effect of social media on our psyches; our understanding of the links between story, groups, and identity in the postmodern world; the relationship of a postmodern story in 140 characters to myth, if any; and what it all says about our present and our future.

---

[277] For the purpose of this essay, I will limit specific examples to Twitter; however the concept of "flow" in a social media feed is equivalent to "timelines" on other social media networks such as Facebook.
[278] From "Mythic Analysis," in *Approaches to Media Literacy: A Handbook*, Second Edition, by Art Silverblatt, Jane Ferry and Barbara Finan. Armonk, NY: M.E. Sharpe, 2009, p. 163.
[279] "Twitter." Wikipedia.org. 5 Feb. 2012. http://en.wikipedia.org/wiki/Twitter.
[280] http://mashable.com/2009/11/19/twitter-whats-happening/.
[281] See Visual.ly service.
[282] Definition of meme: "an idea, behavior or style that spreads from person to person within a culture." http://www.merriam-webster.com/dictionary/meme. 16 November 2011.
[283] From pps. 289-290. "Myth and Mass Media" by Marshall McLuhan. In *Myth and Mythmaking*, edited by Henry Murray. New York: George Brazilier, 1960, pps. 288-299.
[284] McLuhan, "Myth and Mass Media," p. 297.

[285] Frank Rose, *The Art of Immersion: How the Digital Generation is Remaking Hollywood, Madison Avenue and the Way We Tell Stories*. Norton: New York, 2011, p. 203.
[286] Rose, p. 204.
[287] Rose, p. 205.
[288] Rose, p. 220.
[289] "Confession of a Tweeter" by Larry Carlat. 11 November 2011. *The New York Times*. http://www.nytimes.com/2011/11/13/magazine/confessions-of-a-tweeter.html.
[290] As Carlat notes, this is a large number for a non-celebrity.
[291] "Confession of a Tweeter" by Larry Carlat.
[292] "Attention Spans Have Dropped from 12 Minutes to 5 Minutes: How Social Media is Ruining Our Minds" by Neil Vidyarthi. 14 December, 2011. http://socialtimes.com/attention-spans-have-dropped-from-12-minutes-to-5-seconds-how-social-media-is-ruining-our-minds-infographic_b86479.
[293] Charlie Arthur, @numinousviews. Cited with permission. 24 Jan. 2012. http://twitter.com/#!/Numinousviews/statuses/161814278591102976.

23) On the Fortieth Anniversary of Title IX: Female Athletes in Sacred Stories

(Note: This essay was originally published with a different title on April 18, 2012, in On The Issues Magazine, Spring 2012 issue, ontheissuesmagazine.com.)

The physically talented woman-competitor is an amazing feature of many timeless tales.

She runs faster than all the men. She draws the arrow from her quiver, aims and hits her mark perfectly, every time. She swims without fear in the stormy sea. She vaults so high she can nearly touch the sun. She dances with enough force to make thunder. The powerful archetype of the female athlete has many names and thrives in cultural traditions worldwide.

We know about real-world female athletes from the history of the Olympics in Greece, first held in honor of the god Zeus. Female athletes are also woven through myth and folklore; they are divine characters and their desires, feats and follies tell us what it means to be human. They represent behavior so "true" that it helps to define who we are today—an old tale, but evergreen.

One historical story from the original Olympics and six representative sacred stories from Greek, Chinese, First Nation and Yoruba traditions explore the significance of the female athlete as a symbol of strength, determination and extraordinary ability.

1. **First Olympics.** As early as the sixth century B.C., women were running competitively.[294] History tells us that female athletes raced each other in early Olympic games, which were founded to please the gods. The Heraea (or Heraia)[295] was a foot race that predated or coincided with the ancient Olympics. The Heraea was comprised of contests in three different age categories for women, who ran in honor of the goddess Hera. The prize: to become her official priestess. In the stadium at Olympia, women competed wearing tunics, hair down, on a slightly shorter track than the men's course.[296] Although some writers describe a "No Woman" rule at the ancient Olympics, other literature challenges the accuracy of that interpretation.[297]

But it is historically factual that Cynisca became the first woman athlete in history to win in the ancient Olympics as a charioteer in 396 B.C. and winning again in 392 B.C.[298] Cynisca was immortalized in a bronze statue at the Temple of Zeus. Eurylonis, another female charioteer from ancient Greece, became the second crowned female winner; in Sparta, she, too, was memorialized with a statue.[299]

2. **Greek Heroine, Atalanta.** Atalanta is the heroine of Greek mythology who could run faster than all of the men. She began life as a royal princess, but because the king only wanted sons, the tiny infant was left in the forest to die. A mothering bear kindly fed Atalanta until

she was discovered by a group of hunters. They raised the girl as one of their own. After growing up in the wilderness where she ran freely, Atalanta became a renowned huntress and athlete. Atalanta was a key player in the Hunt for the Calydonian Boar,[300] winning its skin; at funeral games in Pelias' honor, she won other games—either racing or wrestling, depending on the version of the myth.[301]

By this time, her father, the king, had rediscovered her, and demanded that she, as princess, be wed at once. But Atalanta wanted to remain single, so she announced to the world that she would only marry a man who could beat her in a race. And there was a catch: any suitor who tried to best her and failed would be killed immediately. Even these extreme proclamations and conditions did not deter potential suitors. Many men died trying to win the athletic princess' hand; Atalanta would give them a head start and they'd still lose. She'd spear them after she caught up with them. It wasn't until Aphrodite intervened, giving the Golden Apples of Hesperides to Melanion to use in the race as tools of distraction, that Atalanta lost a race, and subsequently married.

3. **Lady of the Bow, Artemis.** Some accounts say that the gentle female bear who suckled Atalanta was the goddess Artemis in disguise;[302] Atalanta was devoted to the deity. Artemis was known by many epithets, such as "Lady of the Bow" and "Lady of the Wild Beasts."[303] Like her twin brother Apollo, Artemis was an expert archer, and could use the bow and arrow to kill. Once, Orion angered the goddess; he challenged Artemis to a discus-throwing contest. Artemis killed him, either by

hitting Orion with a discus or, in other versions, by sending a poisonous scorpion his way.[304]

There are many Artemisian myths set in the woods, related to hunting: the story of Actaeon is one of the most famous. Artemis magically turned the hunter into a stag for revenge. Why? Because he broke the rules: he spied on the virginal goddess and her acolytes while they were bathing in a spring. To complete her vengeance, she turned Actaeon's own pack of hunting hounds loose upon him. They devoured the stag.

4. **The Amazons**. Artemis, obvioulsy a fierce opponent, was also the sacred protectress of the Amazons, the legendary matriarchal collective of independent women in Asia Minor (or Libya) known for their astounding physical prowess, equestrian skills, battle command and intolerance of men. The Amazons were renowned archers and expert riders; by legend, these women were the first people to ride horses.[305] One of their famous Queens was Otrera.[306] In art, circa 470 B.C., they were depicted wearing trousers.[307] The Amazons, as a mythological construction, resonate so strongly with the modern psyche that debates continue about their historical existence.[308]

5. **Beloved Goddess of the Sea, Mazu**. In Asia, the deity Mazu is a beloved goddess of the sea and a guardian of sailors, part of Buddhist and Taoist traditions.[309] Today, she is one of the most popular deities in China and beyond, with over one hundred million worshippers worldwide.[310]

As an athlete, she was a swimmer. According to tradition, she was born on March 23, 960, with the name

Lin Mo Niang (or Lin Moniang). Her father and brothers were fishermen, and Lin Mo Niang would stand guard on the shore, wearing bright red garments, to guide fishermen safely back to port. She performed this duty even during terrible storms. One day, her family did not come back from a fishing trip. Accounts differ as what actually happened next. In one version, Lin Mo Niang went into a trance, and in a shocking vision, saw her father and brothers dangerously awash in a typhoon. Lin Mo Niang could visualize helping them, but her mother interrupted the trance. Eventually, some of her family, but not all, returned home safely. In another story, she died swimming, heroically trying to save her lost father.

6. **The Woman Who Leaps.** The sacred Paiute story from North America, "The Woman and the Giants," features a pole-vaulting female who jumps great distances in order to escape bloodthirsty monsters.[311] Two different giants, Tse'nahaha and Pu'wihi, attack a group of indigenous people. The first one, Tse'nahaha, had a look that could kill and many people died from his glance. The Woman was able to hide from Tse'nahaha and tried to save a baby. The encounter with the second monster, Pu'wihi, forced the Woman to jump. As she tricked the second monster toward a burning house, the Woman dug her stick into a wild oats patch, and vaulted high in the sky, landing near a rock formation, where she hid. Pu'wihi eventually found her, but rested a night before attempting to kill her. This next time, the Woman planted her vaulting stick on the rock, so the direction of her jump could not be tracked. The Woman vaulted east to her aunt's house, perhaps miles, where she was out of

danger. The entire Paiute tribe descended from the legendary jumping Woman.[312]

7. **Warrior and Dancer Oya.** Oya is an Orisha,[313] a weather-warrior spirit in the Yoruban tradition, originally associated with the River Niger. She has been merged via Santeria with the Catholic figure, "Our Lady of Candelaria." Oya is so awe-inspiring that when she dances, she creates tornados, thunder and hurricanes. Her flowing skirt creates wind storms and, as a goddess of the elements, fire is also in her control.[314]

Oya is a bringer of change and transformation, often through destruction first, and she guards the entrance to the underworld and cemeteries. A shapeshifter, she can magically transform herself into a water buffalo. Skilled in combat, she fought alongside her husband, Chango (or Sango), in war. Oya is also a lover of truth,[315] and in Yoruba, her name is translated as "She Tore."[316] By some, Oya is thought to be a Spirit of the gym today.[317]

The archetype of the Female Athlete has made a permanent impression in the human psyche. Seen in sacred myths and folktales across traditions and time, she is an inspirational figure who mirrors back to us the potency of women. The strong female athelete that we meet in these tales is not so different from the women on fields and ball courts today—possessed of amazing achievements, physical prowess, an innate desire to compete, and a determination to fight for her people and her causes.

---

[294] "Ancient Olympic Games." Wikipedia. Wikipedia.org. http://en.wikipedia.org/wiki/Ancient_Olympic_Games.
[295] "History of the Olympic Games." Welcome to Athens: Athens and Olympic Games Guide.

http://www.akropol.net/olympic_games_history/history_olympic_games_page.htm.
[296] Golden, Mark. *Sport and Society in Ancient Greece.* Cambridge University Press, 1998. Page 125 (citing Pausanias 5.16.2-4).
[297] "The 'No Woman Rule' in Ancient Olympiads: Macho Myth or Reality?" From *Olympica Hippica: Men, Women, Horses and Mules in the Ancient Olympics* by Theodore G. Antikas. Euandros, 2004. http://users.forthnet.gr/kat/antikas/Chapter6.htm.
[298] "Cynisca." Wikipedia.org. http://en.wikipedia.org/wiki/Cynisca.
[299] "Euryleonis." Wikipedia.org. http://en.wikipedia.org/wiki/Euryleonis.
[300] "Atalanta." Theoi Greek Mythology: Exploring Mythology in Classical Literature and Art. http://www.theoi.com/Heroine/Atalanta.html.
[301] Grimal, Pierre. *The Dictionary of Classical Mythology.* Blackwell, 1996. Page 65.
[302] Others say that the bear was a symbol of Artemis, such as Robert Bell's *Women of Classical Mythology*, Oxford University Press, 1991. Page 73. These variations show that Atalanta was under Artemis' protection.
[303] Grimal, Pierre. Page 62.
[304] Grimal, Pierre. Page 61.
[305] Bell, Robert. Page 30.
[306] "Otrera." Theoi Greek Mythology: Exploring Mythology in Classical Literature and Art. http://www.theoi.com/Heroine/AmazonOtrera.html.
[307] See a vase in the British Museum: http://en.wikipedia.org/wiki/File:Amazon_trousers_BM_VaseB673.jpg.
[308] For one example, visit "The Straight Dope" and the article "What's up with the Amazons" by Ed Zotti (as "Bibliophage"): http://www.straightdope.com/columns/read/2133/whats-up-with-the-amazon.
[309] "Mazu (goddess)." Wikipedia.org. http://en.wikipedia.org/wiki/Mazu_(goddess).
[310] "Mazu: Chinese Goddess of the Sea." Goddessgift.com. http://www.goddessgift.com/goddess-myths/chinese-goddess-mazu.htm. For more on the transnational popularity of Mazu, see "Creating a Transnational Religious Community: The Empress of Heaven and Goddess of the Sea, Tianhou/Mazu, from Beigang to San Francisco" by Jonathan H.X. Lee. Pages 166–183. In *Religion at the Corner of Bliss and Nirvana: Politics, Identity and Faith in New Migrant Communities*, edited by Lois Ann Lorentzen, Joaquin J. Gonzalez, Kevin M. Chun, and Hien Duc Do, Duke University Press, 2009.
[311] "The Woman and the Giants." Paiute Indians: Native American Indians. http://paiute.net/the-woman-and-the-giants.

[312] See also "The Woman and the Giants" at Burns Paiute Tribe website: http://www.burnspaiute-nsn.gov/index.php?option=com_content&view=article&id=52:the-woman-and-the-giants-&catid=35:legends&Itemid=59.
[313] "Orisha." Wikipedia.org. http://en.wikipedia.org/wiki/Orisha.
[314] "Oya." Wikipedia.org. http://en.wikipedia.org/wiki/Oya.
[315] Caputi, Jane. *Goddesses and Monsters: Women, Myth, Power and Popular Culture*. University of Wisconsin Press, 2004. Page 386.
[316] Machacek, David W. and Melissa M. Wilcox, editors. *Sexuality and the World's Religions*. ABC-CLIO, 2003. Page 8.
[317] For one example, see: http://www.tribeofthesun.com/oya.htm.

Pop Mythology—Acknowledgements

To my muses: Jon Wells, The Hamilton Spectator; Phyllis Owens; Alison Stone; Cynthia L. Cooper; Stephanie Pope; David L. Miller; Ginette Paris; Jon Klein; Elizabeth Terzian; Paula Cizmar; David S. Rodes; Robert L. Freedman; Jean Kauffman; Annawyn D. Shamas; Jim E. Shamas; Jim Shamas, Jr.; Annette Shamas; Ellen Shamas-Brandt; Kaylene Wright; Annamarie Wright; Joy Harjo; Gene Toews and Anne Feely; Dori Sippel; Beth Blickers; Brad Wigor; Andraé Gonzalo and Jamie Benson; Carla Cain; Robert Arnold; Bill Adams; Gina Minervini; Susan Cartsonis; Erin Donovan; David Lucas and Jim O'Steen; Deejae Cox and the Los Angeles Women's Theater Project; Adrian Strong; Janeil Swarthout; Jules Aaron; Kathleen Jenks; Velina Hasu Houston; Carol Lipin; Marianne McDonald; Laura Brugnoni; Andi Matheny; Roy S. Johnson; Lynn Montgomery; Brian Nelson; Miriam Braveman; the Klein family; Judy Hunt; Klaus Phillips; Les Hanson; Brett Love; Tom Haun; Jimmy E. Shamas, III; Alec Shamas; Michael Shamas; Mitchell and Sue Lynn Shamas; Emilene Fisher; Jennie Webb; the Los Angeles Female Playwrights Initiative; George Brandt; Burris DeBenning; Mama Mable and Papa; Grandpa and Dolores; Winnie Mae Burris; Leslie Ringold and Marty P.; Fran Ringold; Clarence Major; J.J. DeBenning; Tony Lipin; Pacifica Graduate Institute; the many talented writers who donated their time and talents to Headlinemuse.com; Telemachus Press; those who have employed me as a myth consultant; those who have encouraged me through the many years who are unnamed above. Special mention to Ty Donaldson (buddhacowboy.com), for the beautiful covers. My deepest and profound thanks to you all.

LIST OF ALL ESSAYS AND ORIGINAL PUBLICATION/PRESENTATION DATES

PART ONE—PANTHEON PIECES

1) "Aphrodite and Ecology: The Goddess of Love as Nature Archetype." This essay was first published in *EcoPsychology Journal*, Volume One, Number 2, June 2009. Pages 93–97.

2) "Apollo Updated: *Zero Effect.*" This essay was originally published in *The San Francisco Jung Institute Library Journal* (now *Jung Journal: Culture and Psyche*), November 2000, Volume 19, Number 3, Pages 71–79.

3) "Unseen Beauty: Artemis and Dark Matter" was originally published in *Mythopoetry Scholar*, Volume 2, "Matter and Beauty." Mythopoetry.com. 2 January 2011.
http://www.mythopoetry.com/mythopoetics/scholar11_shamas_artemis.html.

4) "Pieces of Athena (and Her Head)." This essay begins with part of a talk I gave at the Center for Feminist Research, as an Affiliated Scholar from 2003–2004, University of Southern California, Los Angeles, April 21, 2004. The rest is published for the first time in this volume.

5) "Understanding the Myth: Why Cassandra Must Not Be Silenced" This essay was first published in *On The Issues Magazine*, The Café, Summer 2011, on July 13, 2011.
http://www.ontheissuesmagazine.com/2011summer/.

6) "The Hera Factor in Hillary's Run" was originally published in *The Los Angeles Times* on July 11, 1999, pages M3 & M6.

7) "Martha Hearts Hestia" is published for this first time in this volume.

8) "Hygieia and Asclepius: The Holiness of Health" was originally published in *Mythopoetry Scholar*, Volume 1, "Health and Well-Being." Mythopoetry.com, 2 January 2010. http://mythopoetry.com/mythopoetics/scholar09_shamas.html.

9) "Muse-Worthy: Francine Prose's The Lives of the Muses" was originally published in "The Muses," *Spring Journal*, Volume 70, March 2004, pps. 15–23.

10) "America's Zeus." This essay was originally published in *Newsday* on January 14, 2001, with the title "The Clinton Years: America's Zeus," page B5.

PART TWO—MYTH MISCELLANY

11) "The Gaming of Love" was originally published with the title "Love Might Hurt But We Still Like to Watch," *The Los Angeles Times*, August 8, 2000, p. F3.

12) "End Times: Old Problem, New Myth" was originally published with the title "Old Problem, New Myth: Y2K Hype Latest Manifestation of Humanity's Resistance to Change" in *The Los Angeles Daily News*, Viewpoint, Sunday, June 20, 1999, p. 3.

13) "Revolution and the *I Ching*: A Meditation on Hexagram 49" was originally published with a different title in *Mythopoetry Scholar*, Volume Three: "Revolution." 2 January 2012.

http://www.mythopoetry.com/mythopoetics/sch12_shamas_essay.html.

14) "The Trickster and the President" was originally published as "Clinton's Transformation Into Mythical Trickster," Opinion Section, *The Los Angeles Times*, February 7, 1999. Pages M2 and M6.

15) "Hero Worship and the Academy Awards" is adapted from a paper that was first published in the 2004 <u>Society for Interdisciplinary Study of Social Imagery (SISSI) Conference Proceedings</u>: "The Image of the Hero in Literature, Media, and Society," Society for the Interdisciplinary Study of Social Imagery (SISSI). March 18-20, 2004. Colorado Springs, Colorado. Original paper—"Oscar Exemplars: Toward an Exploration of Current Heroes, Hero Worship, and the Academy Awards."

16) "Movies and Creation Myth—*2001: A Space Odyssey*" was originally published as "2001: A Space Odyssey" in film reviews on the "CG Jung Page" in January 2001 at:
www.cgjungpage.org/films/2001odyssey.html.

17) "Entertainment: The Meaning of the Word and Ritual" was originally published as "'Entertainment': A Dirty Word?" Calendar Section, *The Los Angeles Times*, May 1, 2000. It was also incorporated into a paper presented at the Midwest Modern Language Association: "Modern Theatre, Entertainment Ritual and the Theories of Cultural Anthropologist Victor Turner" in Kansas City, Missouri, November 2–4, 2000.

18) "Acts of Protest, Athena, and *Lysistrata*" is published for the first time in this volume.

19) "Matters of the Heart and Soul: Courtly Love" is published for the first time in this volume.

20) "Facing the Dragon: Of Presidential Nominees and Acceptance Speeches" is published for the first time in this volume, and based upon my 2000–2003 study of archetypes and political linguistics in nomination acceptance speeches.

21) "A Few Thoughts on Adaptation" is based on various public lectures and workshops I've given on the topic of myth and fairy tale adaptation, from 1999–2011. See footnote #251 for location specifics.

22) "Swimming in the Tweet Stream" is published for the first time in this volume.

23) "On the Fortieth Anniversary of Title IX: Female Athletes in Sacred Stories" was originally published (with a different title) in *On The Issues Magazine*, Spring 2012, on April 18, 2012. Ontheissuesmagazine.com.